D1426593

IS IT ANTIQUE?

IS IT ANTIQUE?

174 Questions on Antiques
Answered by Leading Valuer

CHARLES F. GILLIARD

Drawings by Chris Evans

LUTTERWORTH PRESS
Richard Smart Publishing

First published 1978

This book is dedicated to my wife, Jane, for all
her encouragement and care since my disablement in
the 1939-45 war

Published by Lutterworth Press
Luke House, Farnham Road, Guildford, Surrey
and Richard Smart Publishing

Copyright © Charles F. Gilliard, 1978

ISBN 0 7188 7019 0

Printed by John G. Eccles
Printers Ltd, Inverness

Contents

Illustrations

INTRODUCTION

The quest for knowledge among the smaller collectors is one of the most encouraging things that has happened in recent years. No longer is antique collecting the prerogative of the few. Interest in our heritage excites both old and young and I have noticed the growing number of young people who now attend auction sales.

Over the past seven years or so, I have been writing the 'Fake or Fortune' page in 'Art and Antiques Weekly' magazine. Readers have sent in queries about articles in their possession, and I have received a volume of letters from many parts of the world as well as Great Britain.

For several months I was presented on a 'radio phone in' programme at the London Broadcasting Company's studio, answering questions from listeners. This encouraged my belief that there is a large number of people interested in antiques and collecting who might welcome information.

In this book I have set out the sort of questions that I am frequently asked in my work as a valuer. I hope the answers I have given will prove informative and help, perhaps, to enable you to identify articles in your possession. Wherever possible questions are illustrated by a drawing or photograph.

I have carefully tried to avoid museum pieces which are beyond the reach of the ordinary collector. The items discussed are the kinds of things that can be acquired from auction rooms and antique shops.

In some cases illustrations have been supplied by auctioneers and private collectors, and while to the best of my knowledge and belief, the photographs used are the copyright of those who supplied them, I must apologise for any accidental violation of copyright, due to change of ownership.

Grateful thanks to the fine art auctioneers Messrs E. Biddle of Biddle and Webb, Birmingham; P.M. Raw of Pearsons, Fleet, Hants; R. Sterry-Ashby of Northampton Auction Galleries, Northampton; Miss B. Walters of Baldwin and Bright, Leominster who supplied and kindly allowed me to use some of the photographs in this book. My thanks also to: Mrs Y. Edwick, Layer Marney, Essex; Miss M.A.V. Gill, Tunbridge Wells; J.K. Mitchell, Chartered Insurance Institute, London; Roy Lakin, Managing Director, Whitefriars Glass, Wealdstone; John Southern, Liskeard; Penny Savage (my sister); Reg, my lifelong friend; and to all those who allowed me to invade their homes, to Andrew Bax and friend John for taking photographs, and to Chris Evans for the line drawings.

Charles F. Gilliard, 1978

1 Collecting

What sort of things should I collect?

The easy answer would be 'Anything', but this would not be helpful or informative. Firstly there is the question of the amount of money that can be spared on what is a hobby, for it will not be a pleasurable exercise if investment is considered too early. Never was there a better quote to bear in mind than 'A thing of beauty is a joy forever!' Do not collect pieces just because they are in fashion because this means an inflated price and may cause you disappointment later. Buy a piece because it pleases your taste, then no matter how the financial world may move, the pleasure remains with you. If the value rises, so much the better.

Personalities differ, and these differences will be manifested in your home by the things you collect. Many people make the mistake of ranging too widely in their choice. Select only a few subjects in order that you may study them because it often pays to specialise.

Strive always to improve the quality of your collection. There is no harm in 'swopping' if it is for the better. Save up to buy something really good. If you can come to a decision fairly early, so much the better, be it furniture, silver, porcelain or pictures. It is also a good idea to have a period in mind on which to base a collection.

Often, by the time one decides on a period, the home is already furnished with basic pieces of furniture. From there on it is a case of carefully blending the old with the new.

There are a number of smaller pieces of furniture from which to choose. For instance, you might start with an attractive (and practical) small circular 19th century table on column and tripod supports. These come in several shades of mahogany and oak.

A bureau is a 'must' and they are not too difficult to find in mahogany or oak. In my opinion, bureaus are still undervalued. The interior fittings will vary; some of the nicer ones have beautiful cabinet work hidden by the slope fall when closed. It is always great fun to discover the secret compartments that some bureaus contain!

The natural follow-up to a bureau is a suitable chair to go with it. There are some quite nice open arm chairs in the Chippendale, Sheraton and Hepplewhite styles. Although late, some of the Edwardian chairs are worth buying and they incorporate much of the earlier influences.

Consider also Victorian coal boxes and commodes which are now having a new lease of life as hide-aways and magazine tables.

A porcelain collection can be both varied and beautiful. Figure groups from a number of factories are very acceptable. Not all

Dresden (Meissen), Derby and other major factory pieces cost the earth and with a little study and experience, good collectable items can be discovered in the most unlikely places. Some pieces have recognisable marks which can be a help, but there are copies which might deceive you. However, many of these are of poor quality compared with the right pieces. It is always advisable, when the opportunity arises, to visit museums and private collections in order to familiarise yourself with the real thing.

Although figures are very attractive, there are other items which are collectable — boxes, vases, table ware and so on — to name but few.

Delft and other pottery have their devotees and fine collections can be built with a little care.

2 Where to Buy?

Where is the best place to buy?

This is a question I am frequently asked. There are several good sources each with their own advantages. The auction room allows one to browse all day on the eve of sale, and there is a catalogue to guide you. Items in which you are interested must be carefully examined for faults and errors of description. The letters a.f. beside an item means that the auctioneer has noticed something wrong, and it is sold as found. Special attention should be paid to the following: examine silver for solder repairs and filling, and furniture for warp, woodworm and bad restoration. Porcelain may be damaged but this fact may be fairly well disguised. No serious buyer should be without a magnifier to help in examination. Good restoration is acceptable especially if the item is rare. THE GOLDEN RULE: never buy anything at auction without viewing. Failure to do this may lead to disappointment and a waste of money.

Mark your catalogue with the maximum price you are prepared to bid and don't exceed it. There is a disease, termed in the trade, 'auctionitis', and if you do not control your bidding you will surely make a hole in your wallet.

Most head porters at auctions are knowledgeable and can be quite useful, but don't worry them with irrelevant questions. They will always bid for you if for some reason you cannot attend, and will expect a small commission for their trouble.

When the sale starts, follow the lot numbers carefully to make sure the lot you are bidding for is the one you want. After the fall of the hammer, the lot on offer belongs to the last bidder. Auctions are governed by the conditions of sale usually printed in the catalogue. The Auction (Bidding Agreements) Act 1927 will be displayed in a prominent place. It is intended to render illegal certain agreements and transactions affecting bidding, but it mainly affects dealers and was introduced to try to prevent the formation of a ring.

Lots purchased are not cleared until the end of sale except by special arrangement. The clerk will present the total account and when receipted this is handed to the porter, who will turn the goods over to you.

Antique shops can be relied upon to display a good selection. You can generally spend time looking round without being worried. There are both general and specialist dealers. The long-established houses know their business. Serious collectors will soon find a shop on which they can rely. Many dealers will discuss your collection and offer good advice, often putting themselves out to obtain some special item for you.

There are other shops which sell almost anything and are often referred to as 'junk shops'. These too are worth a visit and can be a good place to pick up the odd bargain, especially if you arrive just after new stocks have come in.

Jumble sales and charity shops can also turn up some unusual pieces at times. You need to know a little about the subject in order to take advantage of the often quite low prices. Don't be afraid to buy something which looks a bit dirty or is perhaps painted. A good clean up works wonders and can produce quite a nice collector's item in return for the hard work.

Street markets can also provide good pickings but you have to be an early bird to see the best. At one or two markets I know, people arrive before it is barely light.

Vetted Fairs. This means that goods displayed are antique and that the stallholders are generally dealers. Other fairs are now held very frequently in village halls and other venues. These are not usually vetted so you need to have a good look at what you are buying. The goods offered are not necessarily all antiques, but bargains can be picked up by the discerning buyer.

Advertisements in local papers can be tried, but this may involve you in a great deal of wasted time. I always consider this method best left to the trade. When buying from a shop, ask for a receipt describing your purchase. A good dealer is always prepared to do this; it authenticates an item for you and helps as a safeguard for the not too experienced collector.

3 Furniture

In 1950 we bought a marquetry bureau at an auction for fifty pounds and it was thought expensive at the time. It was catalogued antique Dutch. Seemingly the purchase turned out to be a bargain, do you agree?

A Dutch 18th century marquetry bureau

At the time you bought the bureau, marquetry was certainly not the fashion of the day. You were obviously attracted to the very fine craftsmanship and now the bureau has turned out to be a very good investment. That is how collecting should be — attraction first with little thought of investment.

In recent years, pieces like yours have become sought after, and are being returned to the continent where there is at the moment a great demand, particularly in Italy.

Marquetry work was not confined to one country. The Dutch were great masters of the craft, and thus brought about the general term of 'Dutch'. I have often heard English, French and Italian work so called. As a great maritime nation, the ports of Holland imported many exotic woods and these were used in furniture decoration. Marquetry is not an inlay but a veneer, which could be laid on a carcass of much less important wood, forming an inexpensive base on which to work. The task required great skill in cutting wood of different colours which were glued together, Bevel cutting allowed both back and front to be jigsawed together, using both sides to form the pattern required, and gaps were therefore eliminated.

By the end of the 18th century the cabinet industry was still booming with ready markets both in Britain and on the Continent.

Many Dutch craftsmen went to Britain in the 18th century and were gainfully employed making furniture for home use, a little less ornate than the Dutch product which tended to be rather over-decorated.

Recent exporting in quite large quantities will no doubt create a scarcity, and in spite of very tempting offers, sometimes in four figures, the retention of a nice bureau is well worth while.

Marquetry furniture, which in itself provides colourful and attractive decoration, is best displayed against a plain (preferably white), background, to gain the full impact of its beauty.

It would be interesting to know when spinning wheels first appeared. We have a very nice example made in walnut with beautifully twisted turnings. It is in perfect condition and has the patina of an old piece. Could it be 18th century or is it earlier?

An 18th century spinning wheel

It is said the first spinning wheel evolved in India about the 7th century A.D. It was turned with the right hand while the left hand stretched the 'roving' or prepared fibre. In Europe, where they preferred to sit rather than squat on the floor, legs were added to heighten the wheel. Early examples were simple and crude.

The ingenuity of man prevailed and the Saxon wheel came along fitted with a treadle about the middle of the 13th century. The hand driven wheel continued to be used over the years because it was so simple to construct for what was a cottage industry. We must not lose sight of the fact that the simple spinning wheel formed the basis for Hargreaves' spinning Jenny in 1738, which speeded up the process and allowed one person to spin sixteen or more strands at the same time. When Lewis Paul invented his series of variable speed rollers, the hand drawing of roving was superceded and the process speeded up even more. Arkwright's water frame machine of 1769 used the idea with great success. The invention of the 18th century machinery did not prevent the continued use of hand or treadle wheels and they were still used particularly in Wales and Scotland. Cottage and croft spinning and weaving was a source of revenue and continued well beyond the 18th century as a basic industry.

Towards the latter part of the 18th century, the more genteel lady took up spinning as a hobby and it is from this period onwards the more elegant spinning wheels appeared, for the more crude affairs used in kitchens and outhouses would not have been acceptable for use in ladies' drawing rooms. Wheels made by cabinet makers, in keeping with the quality furnishings and mainly in walnut and mahogany, are those which are sought after and find favour among those who collect a piece to stand in the corner of the room today. Some delightful wheels were made in satinwood by John Planta of Leeds, circa 1860 — real treasures, should you be lucky enough to find one of them. The more crudely fashioned items are the result of a wife's demands to her husband for a wheel. A man would have to create from whatever wood he had to hand — elm, beech, oak or pine.

Spinning wheels made before the 18th century are difficult to find. Those that have survived have found their way into museums. Many 18th century pieces show signs of acceptable restoration. Shapes vary quite a bit, there was a basic task to be performed, but the individual makers had their own ideas about the manufacture and personalised styling is much in evidence.

Perhaps worth a mention are the wool winders which were used in conjunction with the wheel. Some, like the wheels, are crudely made, others are fine cabinet-made pieces.

The wheel you have described is late 18th century and a very good example of the drawing room pieces.

We have a circular mahogany table. The edge is slightly raised and the top, which has a raised edge, can be tipped by releasing a brass catch underneath, which is attached to a square block resting on the turned column. The three legs are 'S' curved with rounded toes. Was there a special use for these tables?

An 18th century mahogany tip-top table

Tripod tables came into use round mid-18th century period, about the same time that tea drinking became a social pleasure.

These tip-top tables were used in the drawing room. They could be conveniently tipped when not in use and stood in a corner of the room. The tripod legs allowing for the angle, the piece still remaining attractive to look at.

As in this example some edges were raised or even galleried, no doubt as a safeguard for the fine china used for these tea occasions.

This design is quite simple, some tables were carved and much more elaborate. This example with 'club' toes is circa 1780.

Some of the tables show evidence of the tops and bases being, what we call in the trade, 'married'. (Two tables made into one from damaged pieces. Sometimes the top is later than the base.) It is always a good idea when looking at a table with a view to purchase to look for signs of alteration.

The balance of a table is sometimes upset by marrying. Glance from the edge of the top to the toes — they should be in line — and this is not always so in a married piece.

It is always worth acquiring at least one tea table. They turn up quite frequently at auction and most antique shops have examples on offer. They fit well into most furnishing styles and have many uses.

As you will see from the photograph, this 3 foot 6 inch chest of five drawers has several pieces of veneer missing. It is otherwise quite sound. Is it worth repairing?

A 19th century chest on ogee feet

A 19th century chest of this description is certainly worth the money you may have to spend on it. Restoration by a craftsman does not come particularly cheap, however, and you will get what you pay for. There does not appear to be too much damage. Veneer can be cut and matched. Early veneers are much thicker than the modern machine made counterpart. They were laboriously cut by hand, so you just cannot slip a modern thin machine cut veneer into old pieces. The restorer will carefully select a matching grain and stain it to blend in with the piece on which he is working. Good craftsmen are not easy to find, but are well worth the time you have to wait for their attention.

This is quite a nice looking chest with mahogany 'oyster' veneer on a pine carcass. The brushing slide is an added refinement, for it can also be used as a writing slab. Quartered gunbarrel angles give it a bit of character. The feet are 'ogee', so called because one part is concave, the other convex. The handles would appear to have been changed, and no doubt there is evidence on the inside of the drawer fronts.

There does not seem to be a special use for tall stands these days. What were they used for originally?

In the 17th, 18th and for a good part of the 19th century, these tall stands were an essential part of a room furniture of the larger houses.

Georgian mahogany candlestands

They are simply called 'candlestands' and are the forerunner of the present day standard lamp.

In pictures of interiors, one or more are often seen in drawing and dining rooms, standing in a corner. Early ones tended to be taller and some English examples were quite ornate.

The three illustrated are Georgian period and give a general idea of the styles that can be found in auction rooms and antique shops.

The tops are just wide enough to carry the multi-branched candalabrum for which they were designed. They could be placed in front of wall mirrors for additional reflected light.

These stands can still be used as a display point for candle holders or the later oil lamp. Some of the latter can look quite important shown off in this manner. A vase or ornament can be displayed with advantage in this way — there are few things more attractive than a vase with flower arrangement standing in a corner of the room.

It is interesting to note that posts from canopy beds have sometimes been converted into candle holders. A close examination will reveal a conversion.

Most davenports seem to date in the Victorian period. Were they known before this?

Certainly a large number of davenports are of the Victorian and Edwardian periods, but they were in use before this.

It is generally thought that they took their name from a Captain Davenport, who ordered one to be made in the late 18th century. A small basic chest with writing top and of a portable nature, would certainly have been useful to a military man on his campaigns. We are mostly concerned with their use as a lady's desk.

Early 19th century davenports tended to be fairly plain with tops sliding forward to provide knee space. Some Regency pieces were made in rosewood, with a fret brass gallery at the top. Some

A Victorian walnut davenport

davenports were made with cupboards but most with drawers fitted on one side, balanced with similar false drawer fronts and handles on the other. Fitting drawers at the side, as well as enhancing the look, allowed them to be opened while sitting comfortably in the writing position. They were mainly made as drawing room pieces and therefore were required to be well and attractively made to blend in with other furnishings. Several woods were used, including mahogany, rosewood, satinwood and walnut. The earlier pieces tended to be in rectangular form and the basic design changed little through the century. After about 1830 there was a mood for added adornments, lift-up tops projecting forward to provide leg room and carved, scrolled, or turned leg pillars were added. Feet varied, early pieces having brass castors and later pieces having pottery castors, emphasising the portability for davenports were intended to be easily moved. They can also be found without castors on cheese turned and vase feet and on plinth bases.

From about 1850, highly figured walnut became fashionable and fancy shapes appeared, such as the piano top, looking very like the lid of that instrument. Davenports seemed to have faded away by the end of the Edwardian period and may have been killed off by over-elaborate design. For many years afterwards, pieces hung about on the secondhand market, but in recent years, they have come into demand, and nice examples are sought after by collectors, especially those with fitted interiors.

Some davenports (dare I say it), are a bit on the ugly side, so if you are thinking about buying one, look for something reasonably early, of good design and the best you can afford.

(Incidentally, American readers may call this piece of furniture by a different name, for 'Davenport' in the United States can refer to a sofa or table.)

We have an unusual object which we think might be a pole screen stand. It is painted white on brass. The upright pole has a turned urn finial and three very nicely shaped scroll feet. There is a bell shaped shield piece which can be moved up and down. This has three sets of spikes, presumable for holding the tapestry screen. Are we correct in thinking that it is a pole screen?

I suppose you have got it right, but only in so far as it was used near the fire, but much closer than a pole screen would be placed.

In the 18th century and earlier, small native birds were caught and used as food. Birds such as rooks and sparrows were eaten in the 19th century. In earlier times in Britain, larks were considered a delicacy. The wood lark was widely distributed in large colonies and, unlike some of the other species of larks, was not migratory. It would seem that, under the paint, you have an old brass lark spit or roaster. Most of these are in iron. 18th century brass pieces are rare, so under all that paint hides a collectors' item. Properly cleaned off and polished, it will be restored to give you not only a nice antique, but a conversational piece to stand beside the fireplace. In these days, large open fire places are not much in evidence. If you happen to be fortunate enough to possess one, you could at least use the spit for toasting. I am sure no one would relish impaling tiny birds on in in these enlightened days.

Can a date be given for a rather nice quality stool which has a walnut frame. The frieze is a carved, serpentine shape. The legs are scrolled with oval carved reliefs on the knees.

A Victorian walnut framed stool

A walnut framed stool of this design is Victorian, about 1860. The Victorians favoured ornamentation which was often overdone. In this case it is somewhat subdued; the ears at the top of the scroll supports and the ram's head toes show a generous use of wood. A nice piece of quality cabinet work.

The piano was something of a status symbol in the period and required a nice stool to be placed for use with it. There were also similar wider stools, used as duet stools in the days when a family were required to provide their own entertainment. It was often the practice for children to sit at the piano for the entertainment of visitors.

These stools are worth their place in a furniture collection and although many are used at the dressing table, rather than the piano, they also look well in the drawing room, that being their original place.

Perhaps you would advise us about a mahogany table which we are not too sure about. The diameter of the top is 21 inches and the base 18 inches extended, with three block feet. The whole is 28 inches high. The top is fixed with a rather heavy rectangular block. Do you think it is a genuine piece?

A mahogany occasional table

I feel that you already have some suspicions about the tea table. It depends what you mean by genuine. The top appears to be 19th century and from a table of that period — but it has certainly been, what we call in the trade, married. The base is out of proportion and without the added block feet the table would topple over quite easily. The heavy block under the top is out of keeping. If you examine under the top you will no doubt see evidence of another type of fitting such as screw holes. I think you have a genuine 19th century table top, fitted to a not-so-genuine base, which might well have been part of a lamp standard of later date. It is not unusual to find married tops and bases in these small tables.

So you really have something which is neither here nor there, but made up as it is, it will still provide a useful occasional table.

A friend has sold me a work table, which she said was antique. The wood is mahogany. The top has a flap which can be raised at each end, and it has two drawers at the front with turned wood handles. Under the drawers there is a half circular pleated silk bag which can be pulled out. The centre leg is a carved vase shape, with four scroll legs which have brass leaf ends with casters. Can you date it, and was I wise to pay £100 for the table?

A Georgian mahogany work table

You have acquired for yourself a very nice quality late Georgian style work table in one of the most sought-after shapes. Your friend is quite correct to say it is antique, for it dates just pre-1850. You were very lucky to have it offered to you at the figure you mention and would have been foolish had you missed the opportunity to buy this fine ladies' table, which is original in every respect.

These pieces are now fairly rare and the value rises quite substantially every year.

In these days when the lady no longer sits with her table beside her, working fancy stitches, the table can still make its attractive contribution in any furnishing style. It can be put to several uses and still remain a pleasure to behold.

We have a small nursing chair. It has quite a high back with an upholstered top piece. The seat is low and padded, with some carving on the front. The legs are short cabriole with carving and have white china castors. Is it antique?

A Victorian 'prie-dieu'

Firstly, let me say that this is not really a nursing chair, albeit admirably suitable for that purpose. It is known as a 'prie-dieu', the name taken from the French, meaning praying desk. It is one of the special purpose pieces intended for use, (usually by the lady of the house), for daily devotions. Mainly made in walnut, mahogany or rosewood, some have a small box fitted on the back of the upholstered crest rail intended for the storage of a prayer book, and the tiny daily prayer scrolls, which are rarely found now. A scroll was selected at random to be read. I remember my grandmother's scroll box in the 1920's but have not seen one since.

These praying chairs follow much in the same style, some more elaborate than others. The French examples are sometimes in Gothic style, with church window backs into which is inserted a painted religious panel, usually Madonna and Child. They seem to be a product of the 19th century, reaching their peak between 1840 and 1870.

This example is English, circa 1865, with the French style cabriole leg. The porcelain castors were popular in that period.

Castors have been known from the 17th century when they were made in hard wood. Later came leather discs and by the late 18th and early 19th century they were made in brass and used as a feature for end leg decoration, using cups in leaf, plain or a motif. I have not seen porcelain castors used on legs earlier than 19th century. No doubt, few of these antique prie-deus are used for their original purpose. I fear that in the main they just represent a different and decorative piece of furniture and are often mistakenly called nursing chairs.

We have an old oak two-piece lofty corner cupboard. The doors are inlaid with strips of walnut. There is a little repair required. Would it be worthwhile to have this done? Would the bottom piece have had feet originally?

Hanging corner cupboards

This type would not have had feet for rather than a two-piece cupboard, you actually have two hanging cupboards which have been, what the trade terms, 'married'. The base is different and the doors would have been crossbanded in the same way, not one round the edge, the other within the edge. They should really be treated as separate pieces made in the 18th century.

Antique pieces are generally worth restoring providing the work is put in the hands of experienced craftsmen. Bad restoration can do more harm than good. Corner cupboards mostly date from the beginning of the 18th century. They were in use before, but it was the Dutch importations which brought them to popoularity, William and Mary period.

They are seen with straight fronts as hanging or standing cupboards, also the lofty ones in one piece, or matching pieces placed one on the other. The bow fronts were made by glueing several strips of wood, chamfered together. This can be seen in oak pieces and hidden by veneer in mahogany or walnut cupboards.

Some corner cupboards have glazed doors, the glass in small panes, supported by strips called astragals, which are attached to the surround frame.

If the door has a single sheet of glass, with astragals on the outside and inside, it has been replaced, or the piece is later than early 19th century date. There is nothing against using unmatched cupboards, one on the other, for convenience sake. It is not always possible to find two uncluttered corners in a room, on which to hang cupboards. When hanging corner cupboards, care must be taken to make them really secure, bearing in mind the added weight which will ensue from glass and china which will be placed in them.

Quite a range of corner cupboards can be found to blend in with any furnishing taste.

Pilasters are generally thought to add quality to the piece. 'H' hinges were used by country craftsmen around mid-eighteenth century.

Would it be possible to date a walnut card table? The top flaps over in the usual way, but it does not have the swing leg support. Both rear legs are attached to a section of the frame which is pulled out. It has oval wells which are used for counters. We are not quite sure about the circular pieces on each corner. Were these used for drinking glasses? It has rather heavy cabriole legs, with carved shell knees and ball and claw toes at the front.

A walnut card table c. 1728

This is a very nice example of an early card table in walnut which dates circa 1728.

You are quite correct about the wells to hold each players counters or in some cases guineas. The circular trays in each corner were for the silver candlestick. In these days, when the flick of a switch produces light, we tend to lose sight of the lighting problem of earlier times, when the candle played its part.

Card tables were known in the 17th century but it was the 18th century which brought them into prominence. Gambling was rife among the gentlemen of quality. These specially designed tables were found in most residences of the gentry.

They were occasional pieces and the fold-over tops allowed them a dual purpose role as a side table when closed. This is also the reason for the more elaborate front feet which we often see.

The single leg support for the opened top was a little unstable. The concertina frame, as it is called, allowed not only stability, it also gave a more symmetrical proportion when open.

It is always interesting to note the generous use of wood in early cabriole legs which allowed deep carving at the knees and really powerful toes.

In the early 18th century, most tables were of rectangular form, however there did appear some circular designs often seen with double flap tops. The second flap could be lifted to reveal a deep well for the storage of gaming materials.

Later in the century, more circular types appeared in very pretty designs, sometimes in pairs, one with a polished inner top for use as a tea table. When not in use, these were often placed as pillar tables. Most antique card tables are attractive pieces of furniture and still have practical present day use.

Is it possible to date a small mahogany three-tier table? The height is 28 inches and it is 13 inches deep. The rectangular shelves are supported on four gun barrel turned supports with mushroom type finials. The feet are bun shape and each has a brass castor. This was bought very cheaply in a market in a dirty and paint-splashed condition. It has been cleaned and waxed and is of even colour with a good shine.

All of which only goes to prove that the odd bargain can still be found! This table comes in the category of a 'whatnot'. These came into use about 1760 and the early pieces were fairly tall and tapering. This one of later date, circa 1820, is of the lower variety which can be so useful. They are ideal as a magazine table, for display of ornamental pieces or bedside table. This is a well-proportioned piece, suitable in most furnishing surroundings. Whatnots can be found in a variety of shapes and sizes, some with one or more drawers. They come up quite frequently in auctions and it is worthwhile to acquire at least one example.

We would like to know the date of a Windsor armchair. The back, (in two sections), has a carved open splat with spindles below the arms, stick turnings above. It is quite solid looking and heavy, but is not of oak. Is it 18th century?

A 19th century Windsor armchair

The Windsor chair is not as early as 18th century but of the later 19th century mechanical age. The stump turnings at the front, supporting the arms, were baluster turned in this period. The early Windsor arm chairs have a plain turned swept back stump. The design has changed little, in a general sense, over the centuries. They have always been an example of the country craft which produced them — solid and comfortable. The story goes that one day, George I rested in one of these chairs at a country house and was so impressed by the comfortable seat that he ordered a quantity to be made for use at Windsor Castle — thus the name 'Windsor'.

The actual date of origin is difficult to define. They were certainly made before George I period and probably evolved from the 16th century triangular chairs, examples of which still exist.

Early examples with crinoline stretchers and cabriole front legs are those most sought after.

Your chair, in beech wood, is a far cry from those made by the chair makers known as 'bodgers' who set up in the woods of Buckinghamshire. Timber was bought where it stood, and a rather primitive pole lathe erected on site, with a hut for shelter, made of branches and bracken. The craftsman was soon in business.

Windsor chairs were also made without arms and were intended for cottage rooms. Some had splats of varying design, including the wheel which is so well known that they have acquired the name 'wheelbacks'. Most Windsor chairs are made in beech and elm, although other woods are occasionally found, but to find one in yew wood is the greatest joy!

The English country pub is one of the places to see the delightful Windsors, bearing the patina which only a pub chair can achieve. Once plentiful, stocks have been depleted over the past two or three years. Even late 19th century chairs will be hard to find in the very near future, and, consequently, are expensive.

Having three old dining chairs with rush seats and spindle backs in two rows, it would be nice to try and make up the set. The wood is grained but we are not sure about it. Were these chairs usually made in oak?

18th century chairs with rush seats

These are typical country chairs and were popular right through the 18th century. The most common woods used were elm, beech, oak and yew. The design was much the same all over the country, particularly the legs, stretcher and toe turnings. Some were made with spindle backs, others, with what we call ladder backs, purely because they resemble that implement.

These chairs have survived in numbers. They are very strong, and were produced on a massive scale for use in the country where the wood used for them abounded, and the rushes readily to hand. The design was simple and easy to produce. It is difficult, due to the long period of production, to date them accurately. Suffice it to say, 18th century in most cases. William Morris re-introduced the design in the 19th century which further extended the use of these chairs.

It would be nice to make up a set of four or six, for it is rare to see them offered in more than singles, twos, and occasionally threes.

They are more likely to be found in the smaller country auctions or shops. Lancashire and Wales are probably the best areas to search, but they do turn up almost anywhere.

Can you define the purpose for which a mahogany table was intended? It is 4 foot long by 2 foot wide. The centre of the top is hinged to a section of the frame and can be raised to a graduated slope. The legs are turned with matching balls at the top and bottom.

A 19th century artist's table

During the 18th century, tables appeared which were made for a specific purpose. Card and tea tables are examples.

The architect's or artist's table came on the scene about 1720. In the early pieces, the working top was pulled out from a chest with a false top drawer. When returned, the legs formed pillars. The designers soon recognised the potential and tables were made with tops which could be raised to varying heights.

Tables designed by men like Chippendale are a joy to see. They are graceful pieces of furniture made to match the other house furniture, with all the refinements, elaborate fret decoration, candle slides and so on, fit to grace the drawing rooms of the period. These pieces were also adaptable for reading. During the 19th century there was a great interest in drawing, and the period produced many artists in the amateur field. (This is in evidence today from the number of water colour drawings which are available — some quite talented work.) A straight-forward drawing table which could also be used as a side table was more in demand, and this example, about 1840 date, is representative. Some of the late 18th and early 19th century tables appear to have been designed with the lady in mind, and are very pretty pieces in Sheraton style.

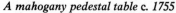

Is it possible to find the near date of a beautiful and unusual mahogany tea table? The circular top is 22 inches in diameter with a dished edge carved in dragoon work. The central pillar is beaded, the baluster open and pear shaped. Four slender scrolls with cartouche support the top. It has three shaped legs which are finely carved with leaf, scroll and bluebell. The toes have generous whorled proportions. The table is 28 inches high. The piece was acquired about twenty years ago.

A mahogany pedestal table c. 1755

You certainly have a most exquisite antique pedestal table dating circa 1755. A piece of this description can be considered quite rare. It is a fine example of a purpose-made small table and the craftsman, (whoever he was), must be admired. Such a pity that so little English furniture carries a signature!

It is usual for most mid-Georgian furniture to be tagged with the Chippendale label — it is an embracing term. This piece can deservedly be called so in the manner of that great craftsman designer. The flowing form is typical of some of the styles shown in Chippendales' book *The Gentleman and Cabinet Makers Director*. Thomas Chippendale's own cabinet work was superb, but, there are not too many examples which can be documented as by his hand. Fortunately, now and again items are found among the collections in our great houses and a search in the archives has produced the acknowledgment of the order or a receipt.

I can think of no collector who would not envy your possession, which, if it ever came to the market, would cause quite a stir. Very rarely is such a piece on offer. I can understand why you became attracted to it in the first place.

Buying at the time you did, has not only given you a joy to live with, but also an investment of some proportion which was probably far from your mind at the time.

Here we have a prime example of advice often given, to buy something good, rather than follow the fashion of the day and often live to regret spending money on something of inferior quality.

We have been looking for a set of six antique dining chairs, to match a two-pillar dining table in mahogany which we already possess. We think it dates circa 1800. Among the effects of a relative were six mahogany chairs and two footstools. We took the opportunity to purchase for the probate value. The chairs have circular backs with two small raised carvings and the cabriole legs have carvings on the knees. The stools are quite pretty with carved rosette frieze and short scroll feet. Do you think these chairs really go with the table or should we sell them?

You have been quite fortunate to have the chance to buy at a probate value. The chairs are of the balloon back style and date circa 1850. Earlier Victorian furniture retained some of the French style for a while and then became much heavier and more bulky in design — 'good solid stuff', as they used to say. These have the genteel look and are quite a bit later than the table, but antique never the less.

If you wish to be nearer the mark your search must continue, for, I would think, a Sheraton design. It might still take some time to achieve your object and it would be advisable to retain the balloon

A Victorian balloon back chair and footstool

back set until you do. They will grow on you as they are a desirable set and of course their value will no doubt increase with each year. You may never want to part with them. The pair of footstools have their value and a reminder of the days when floor draughts were prevalent. They have now become collectors' items and it is fairly rare to find a matching pair.

Can you explain the original use of a bow fronted corner stand? The wood is mahogany. It has a raised back. The top has a circular piece let into it in a different grained wood, which looks like walnut. The centre shelf has a small drawer; the bottom shelf is smaller and attached to the curved out legs with struts.

This piece is without doubt a Georgian corner washstand. The circular inlay you mention is a later addition, its purpose to fill the hole in which the washbasin rested. Toilet requisites were kept in the drawer, the ewer standing on the bottom shelf. The china for these pieces was usually smaller than the normal and occasionally you do come across a set, often made in ironstone and quite decorative. The back acted as a splash back to protect the decorations. Washstands were mainly a guest bedroom furnishing where the room did not contain the often larger marble topped washstand. With modern plumbing, the washstand is an obsolete item, but many of the prettier ones can be adapted to alternative use, your own, for instance, providing a useful corner piece for display purposes, in other words an attractive 'whatnot'.

Can you supply information about a walnut chest which is quite old? It is 38 inches wide. The top folds and when opened is supported on two pull-out slides similar to those on a bureau. There are two short and three long drawers of different depth. The edges of the drawers are raised and there is a banding round them. The handles and keyhole covers are in brass with shaped plates which have a slight chasing. The feet are of the bracket type and it is in perfect condition.

A George I walnut bachelor chest

This is a very choice chest of sought-after size, known as a 'bachelor'. It has nicely figured walnut veneer which is hand cut and is much thicker than the machine-made veneers. The drawers have integral cockbead edges moulded from the piece, rather than added strips often seen in later antique pieces. The carcass is probably pine. Cross banding is always an asset and adds to the value. The handles are original. One often finds they have been changed to keep up with fashion. You have not mentioned if the locks are intact — perhaps that is too much to hope? The fold-over top adds to its charm as well as an additional use as a writing table. The slightly fretted bracket feet are in good proportion. This country-made chest is George I period, circa 1720. Such a great pity that we shall never know who made this quite valuable piece.

I had always admired a china cabinet which stood in my grandparents' home and it was eventually left to me. I do not know anything about antique furniture and would like to know a little about the cabinet. It is 48 inches wide and just over 5 feet tall. The wood is red mahogany with a light colour inlaid in patterns and lines. The glass side windows are curved and the two shaped doors have moulded strips over the glass. There is a shaped shelf underneath between the six slender square legs, which have small shaped ends. Can you help?

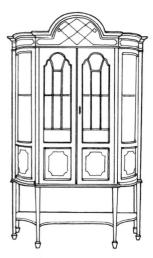

An Edwardian display cabinet

You have an eye for a nice piece and these cabinets were well produced. It will still be a few years before they can be classed as antique, having been made late in the 19th century. Edwardian cabinets have come into some favour of late and are destined to become the collected antique of the future, not too distant, I might add. They have the graceful lines of the much earlier Sheraton pieces. The bow glass side panels which might prove a problem if broken, follow on from the Victorian credenza which is often seen with them. You have not mentioned the lining, this is usually in silk tapestry and also covers the shelves. The door mouldings on this piece are termed astragals, and are purely for decoration and to simulate the appearance of the 18th century cabinets, in which the glass was in small panes puttied in to the astragals which formed part of the door frames. The satinwood inlay stringing adds tone and the square taper supports with spade toes are in the Sheraton tradition. These cabinets will increase in value over the next few years.

Can you possibly date an old oak armchair which was bought at a country farm auction some years ago? It is very solidly made and quite heavy to move. The back is panelled and carved with flowers and leaves and has a scrolled carved top. The arms are very solid and slightly serpentine in shape and supported on turnings which have a block centre supporting the seat before continuing as a leg. The front of the seat, which is plank, is carved in a series of arches. The rear pegs and stretchers are square, slightly chamfered at the top and show signs of wear. I hope this will prove sufficient information?

17th century wainscot chairs

Very well described, if I may say so, and leaves me in no doubt that this is a 'wainscot' chair dating circa 1670. These chairs were made in fair numbers and followed on from the dining bench. Some call them ecclesiastical, but their use was not confined to the bishops. The name wainscot is derived from the room panelling so named — no doubt because the backs are panelled in a similar way and can be carved or plain. The older chairs are often found without carving. The turnings resemble gun barrels, some straight, some slightly baluster in form. These were easy to turn on a pole lathe. The stretchers should show wear in the normal places where the feet were rested to keep off the cold flag floors. Quite often there is evidence of wear on the toes where the wood has been softened by dampness due to the washing of flagstone floors.

These large chairs were made well into the 18th century and were carpenter rather than cabinet-made. Most estates employed a man handy with tools, who could fashion furniture from timber readily available from woods on the estate. These chairs are joined by the peg method which is clearly seen. In spite of the austere look the chairs are quite comfortable. The general characteristic shape changed little over the years. Late reproductions have been made and even though some may have been stressed (in other words faked) there are several signs by which these can be recognised; different methods of assembly were used and evidence of the use of modern tools can be seen. By taking opportunities to examine the genuine, one soon learns to recognise the spurious.

We bought a Windsor armchair at an open air market in Newton Abbot while on holiday in the West Country for only ten shillings, (fifty pence in today's currency). It was painted green, but it was the shape which prompted us to buy it. It has a round seat with the legs placed in the less conventional position with turned crossed stretchers. After getting it home it was stripped of paint which revealed an all beechwood chair. With a few years wear and waxing it has taken on a very pleasant colour. How old would you think it is?

A Windsor corner chair

It is a bit unusual with the legs sited in a similar way to the corner chair, and this chair could well stand in a corner. The earlier arm chairs tended to have arms which gave added strength to the back by continuing round. Although Buckinghamshire is often considered to be the home of the Windsor, they were made by craftsmen all over the country where raw material abounded. This one could well have been made in the Shepton Mallet area where there was a thriving chair centre. Windsors were often travelled by makers' representatives and sold from the waggon in the 19th century. Windsors of the ordinary style are difficult to date or attribute to any particular maker; they were highly commercial and styles varied little. This chair was probably sold in the white for oiling or painting to the whim of the customer, and from the style I would not think it earlier than mid-19th century. You can still buy Windsors in the white but these are machine-made, for gone are the days of the country bodger (who made the turnings) and bottomer (who made the seats).

Having purchased a small table at auction, described in the catalogue as a 'sewing table', I would like to know the period of manufacture. The wood is rather dark with an even darker grain. The top lifts up and it has several compartments. Underneath there is a cloth bag which can be pulled out. The table stands on a single column with four feet. Would this table be antique?

From what you describe, the sewing table is certainly antique and made in rosewood which was quite popular with the early 19th century craftsmen. The small inner compartments intended for sewing things, cottons, silks etc., and often small tools such as thimbles, embroidery scissors and needles. The pull-out bag was used for materials and unfinished work and was very convenient as it tucks well out of sight. The turned pillar support and splay feet give a nice proportion to a piece of furniture, which usually stood beside the lady's chair at the fireside. Consider this to be a good buy. Date, circa 1820. These tables are not too plentiful on the market, and really nice cabinet examples somewhat rare, especially with original accessories in the compartments.

We would like to know the approximate age and use of a small chest of drawers. The wood is mahogany with a shaped grain. The edges of the top are banded, also the three drawers. At the top there is a flat piece of wood which can be pulled out. The feet are shaped and the width is 33 inches.

This piece is known as a 'bachelor's chest'. It is usual to find them in mahogany veneer with crotch graining. The cross banding round the edges is a refinement, and is achieved by laying the veneer in strips. The pullout slab can be used for both writing and brushing. You have not mentioned the handles; these are generally in brass of 'D' form, fixed to lugs which pass through the drawer front and secured by small nuts. The slide handles being small knobs, also in brass. The feet are the bracket type often seen in the second half of the 18th century. The chest dates circa 1770 and was a dressing room piece. These days, they mostly appear to be displayed in the drawing room.

A walnut secretaire chest has been in our family for many years, which I will probably inherit. It is 73 inches tall and 36 inches wide. The top half has two small drawers and two large ones and a drop flap which, when open, is supported on two pull out blocks. The interior has drawers and pigeon holes. The lower part has three long drawers and stands on feet which are slightly shaped. It is said to be 18th century; it is possible to attribute it to a more accurate date than that?

Left, *an early 18th century walnut secretaire chest.* Above, *a similar chest open*

This is certainly a very nice piece of walnut furniture with excellent and fine matching crotch veneer which must of necessity have been cut by hand. The edges are crossbanded, (veneer laid with cross grain), and the stringing, (fine inlaid lines in light wood), is probably hollywood herringbone (chevron lines resembling a fishbone). The pigeon hole arches are still showing Dutch influence and the handles and key plates of the style used early 18th century. This is one of the more rare small width pieces sought after by collectors and it is a pleasure to see one in such prime condition. Feet in this style are called 'bracket' and were much used through the 18th century and beyond, particularly in the Chippendale designs. It is fine craftsmanship when you see such a piece, with beautifully fitted interior and perfectly graduated drawers. The general appearance shows it to be a George I period circa 1715. It is certainly a worthwhile inheritance which can only give pleasure.

I was offered a rather nice little French Boulle desk by a friend and decided to buy it because I liked it so much. She did not know a lot about its history but said it was definitely antique. It has a gilt metal gallery along the top, back and sides and the interior is fitted with drawers and pigeon holes. The flap is deeper than one normally sees on a bureau and is profusely inlaid with brass over a reddish ground. The drawer in the frieze is quite deep and inlaid in the same way. The top section has side handles and can be detached from the table. The woodwork frame is black. The bureau has a line of gilt beads along the top, over the fall, and round the edge of the table, which also has a row of drapery. The legs are cabriole with figure pieces at the top and bead running down to hoof-shape toes. It would be interesting to know about what date it was made, and why it is called Boulle?

A Boulle desk, early 19th century

This Louis type desk followed on as a slight variation to the earlier 'Bureau en das d'ane'. Similar pieces with bookshelf or cupboard on top are referred to as 'Bonheur du jour'. These small desks were designed for ladies and this one dates early 19th century. Black lacquer complements Boulle work and was used in place of the earlier ebony. The original exponent of the work to which he gave his name, was Andre Charles Boulle born in 1642, died 1732. He was 'ebéniste' to King Louis XIV, and ably assisted by the bronzier Jean Caffieri, produced some wonderful work for the royal palaces.

The making of this type of furniture was not easy in those days before the advent of machinery, as you will realise if I explain that a sheet of brass was placed together with a sheet of tortoise shell and both cut into the intricate pattern at the same time, producing two identical pieces; moreover the design in reverse could be used on another piece of furniture to match, hence no waste of material. Boulle work is usually complemented with gilt metal and on special pieces, ormolu was used. Early work can be distinguished by the fine carving on the metal. Later metal work is cast, and rather crude in comparison. The figure head pieces on the knees are called 'caryatides'. Having mentioned the word ebeñiste I should explain this was the name given to a worker in ebony. Later, when the more exotic imported woods were used, an 's' was added. The Guild of Ebeñistes in France wielded nearly as much power as the Guild of St. Luc in the Netherlands. The cabinet trade was jealously guarded by them and in 1741 it was decreed that ebenistes register their marks and sign their work with a metal stamp to prevent foreign competition. J.M.E. was also added to show that it had been vetted by 'Jure des Menuisiers-Ebeñistes'. Pieces found unmarked were treated as contraband, and a fine resulted if put on sale. Pieces can be traced to makers by these marks, but here again there may be fakes.

Reproductions often bear marks but are of such poor quality they should fool no one. An outright forgery is a masterpiece in its own right and was very costly to make so there would not be many such pieces to be found. Boulle work had its period of unpopularity but is back with a vengeance now, particularly on the continent. You should enjoy the use of your desk for many years to come.

We have acquired a small mahogany chest of rather unusual design. It has two short drawers at the top, one of which has a tooled hide top. The handles are of brass and are recessed in the drawer fronts. The angles are protected by strips of brass. It seems to have been cut in half at some time to make two pieces, one on top of the other. We would like to know if it is an antique piece?

This is a piece known as a military chest and was specially made in two sections for ease of carriage. These chests were popular in the early 19th century and were used by officers on a campaign as part of their camp equipment. The covered drawer acted as a writing table but not all these chests have them, although some are found with a pull-out slide. The naval officers had their sea chests also.

The military or campaign chest was made in several woods, camphor, teak, mahogany, oak. Most have brass handles but I have seen recessed turned wood. Two types of feet are found, turned and bracket, some of course sit in a plinth base. Many of the chests have substantial side handles which made moving easier. The small size makes them sought after by collectors, and they do make attractive drawing room pieces. It must be said that, like many pieces, they have been reproduced but these should not fool anyone with a little experience of old furniture.

We own quite a large oak roll-top desk the inside fitted with drawers and pigeon holes. The top lifts off the pedestal bases which have three drawers in each. It is in store at the moment, and we would like to know if it is worth keeping.

There was a time not too long ago when these desks were completely rejected, no interest in them at all. Things have changed and they seem to have found favour now. They were not a general household item, mostly they could be found in doctors' and solicitors' offices. They are quite commodious, and of course have the advantage with the tambour, (slats glued to a piece of canvas) as it can be pulled down to hide the muddle most busy desks get into, including mine. I would say, keep it if you can find room in your home in the near future. Otherwise it might be better to offer it at auction rather than continue to pay storage over a long period. The mahogany types are much more elegant in the home and are more likely to fit in better with your furniture. These usually have cylinder front instead of tambour and are in the main showing more age than the oak examples.

We have recently acquired a bureau. It looks as though it might be Sheraton, but we are not sure. It is veneered with mahogany, inlaid with a lighter wood. The slope flap is inlaid with a shell oval, and there are signs that the hinges have been replaced. The interior has drawer and pigeon holes, but the quality does not match up to the exterior. The three lower drawers are pine and beech lined, handles 'D' shape with plates. There are holes in the inner drawer fronts near the handle fittings. The piece is dented in several places with small burn marks. Do you think it is 18th century?

The interior fittings in old bureaux are generally of equal quality, some with very fine workmanship. If you examine the bottom of the flap where the hinges are fixed, there could well be signs that a new piece has been put in. Damage occurs when pressure is put on the opened flat if the supports have not been pulled out. The dents and burn marks mentioned indicate that the piece has been what we call 'stressed', a process used to give the impression of age, in other words 'faking'. This bureau is Edwardian period and an attempt made to make it look older. The bracket feet are out of proportion and have been added; the handles have also been changed from stamped ovals to Chippendale style. So it is not as old as perhaps you thought, but still a serviceable piece.

A small mahogany antique table has been in our possession for quite a long time. It is only 12 inches square at the top which is surrounded by a low waved edge raised border. There is a pull out slide 4 inches wide in the frieze which has a small brass ring handle. The square legs are tapered ending in spade shape toes. We have often wondered about the original use of this table.

This is a Georgian urn stand dating circa 1780. They were used in the drawing room. A beverage was prepared and put into the urn in the kitchen. The urn was then brought to the room and placed on the table, which was placed convenient to the mistress, who then served her guests. The pull-out slide was used to hold the cup and saucer while pouring. The raised gallery top prevented accidents by keeping the urn in place. Sometimes the table was used as a spirit kettle stand. The urn table is reminiscent of genteel living and not a great many have survived.

The urn table can still be used as a chairside coffee table, or a stand for lamp or jardiniere. It would be nice if you could find a nice antique plate or copper urn to display the original use.

We have a very well made piece of mahogany furniture which we have always called a washstand. The piece stands 32 inches high and has a circular moulded hole in the top, 11½ inches in diameter, which was intended to hold the washbowl. The top is supported on three slender baluster turned pillars fitted into a triangular box with two drawers. The pillars continue below this to a triangular base with shaped edges and three shaped legs with club toes. In the base there is a recess circle presumably for holding the water jug. It does seem a bit small for a washstand; was it put to some other use? We have often thought of having a top put on it as it would make a pretty little table.

This is not exactly a washstand although it had a toiletry use. These pieces were a necessary accessory to the gentleman's dressing room in past centuries. In early times, wigs had been worn by Egyptians, Persians and others, but it was King Louis XIII, (1610-1643), who created the fashion among gentlemen by wearing a wig to cover his baldness. Louis XIV's period saw a greater elaboration, and enormous hair pieces, draping the shoulders became the fashion. In England the full bottomed wig, as it was called, was used up to about 1660. After that the smaller 'peruke' tie wig became the order of the day. Wigs required to be kept in presentable order and were brushed and powdered with flour, and other white powder. You have quite a nice example of a Georgian stand made for that purpose. A bowl occupied the top; the powder receptacle was kept on the base and the two drawers housed implements and perfumes.

A Georgian mahogany wig stand

Towards the end of the 18th century the wearing of wigs subsided and natural hair was powdered.

Sometimes these stands have an additional fitting to hold the wig. Most would have contained a silver or pewter bowl. An ironstone or porcelain example looks quite well and can be used to some advantage for a floral display. Any temptation to fit table tops should be resisted as these items are becoming something of a rarity and should be preserved in original condition.

We have a good plain antique oak stool. The legs are turned in a slightly bulbous gun barrel style, with stretchers all the way round. It has ball shaped feet which show a little sign of wear. From what period were these stools used?

Stools of some sort or other go back for centuries; they can even be seen in early Egyptian sculptures. The stool described was used from the Stuart period and many 17th century pieces have survived. This stool is known as a joined stool, held together by pegs hammered into special holes made by a pegging iron. Pegs hold fast and were much more efficient than nails; they were cut across the grain, which prevented shrinking. Often in old pieces the pegs are seen to stand proud — the carcass wood, not the pegs, has shrunk. Like modern chairs, stools were made in sets to be used with the heavy oak dining tables. When not in use it was the practice to lay them down under the table, the frieze resting on the table stretcher, no doubt so that they were out of the way when clearing and laying the board. I have been asked why stretchers on early tables are so near the floor. I do not think the main object was for the storing of stools. We have to bear in mind that many floors were flags, or even dirt covered with rush; these would strike cold to the feet and the stretcher was used to keep the feet off the floor.

Not all joint stools are as old as they might look. There are those which have been faked to look antique in devious ways such as fuming with sulphur to obtain an aging colour, hitting with chain and hammer, grooving edges and stretchers to simulate wear, assembly with glue and screw, afterwards covering the countersunk head with a mock peg. If a stool looks suspicious and you feel that it has been what we called 'stressed', examine it closely. In normal use, wear will not be symmetrical. Fakers often make the mistake of simulating wear in too uniform a fashion, and in places where it could not possibly occur. Wear on the feet is really difficult to fake. Move a chair or stool yourself and you will find the action shows that, over a period of years, wear could not possibly be symmetrical on all four feet, but there would be some wear caused by dragging.

Some joint stools are found with genuine old bases and replacement tops. This reduces value. Turn a stool over and evidence of replacement often presents itself in the colour. There is often the evidence that the new top has been screwed from the top and the heads concealed with mock peg or filling. Old pegging was done from the underside.

Joint stools were reproduced on into the 18th century and these later pieces are the more easily found. The most desirable stools are those 17th century pieces with 'H' form stretchers and bobbin turned legs. A closed stool, one with enclosed sides in 17th century oak, is fairly rare. These were used to house the pewter chamber pot; it may seem strange to us now, but these were also kept in the living rooms!

Some joint stools have been referred to as 'coffin', no doubt because a pair would be convenient for supporting a coffin resting in the house before burial, but there is no evidence that they were made for that specific purpose.

We have a small chest of four drawers; it is only 25 inches wide. We are not sure about the wood from which it is made; perhaps it is mahogany but it is rather red and the grain is not quite the same as in our other mahogany pieces. The drawers are lined with pine and have slightly raised edges. The handles are brass and quite large in comparison with the size of the chest and the plates over the keyholes are similar. The feet are slightly shaped and of the bracket type. Can you suggest the wood from which it is made and the date of it?

This is a very pretty country chest of the most desirable size. Not many of these small ones come on the market these days and are, in fact, fairly rare. From the description, the wood is red walnut, not often encountered. The drawers are nicely graduated without adorn-

A red walnut chest c. 1740

ment apart from the raised edges, which are called 'cockbead'. These small chests are sometimes termed 'bachelor'. The handles, escutcheons and plates are rather large but they look original and make a nice feature.

Made by a craftsman, more carpenter than cabinet maker, using solid plank rather than veneer to fashion a piece worthy of its place in an antique furniture collection. The date, circa 1740.

About fifteen years ago while on holiday in Scotland, we visited an auction and bought a pair of standard chairs. They have oak frames with drop-in seats, the legs are square with spindle stretchers. The backs are very high with two splats and three small squares pierced in each. The top rail is also pierced with a hand hold. The unusual design attracted us to them, and at the time we thought they were antiques. We now have doubts; what do you think?

The chairs have a distinctive design and are not antique but they do not have too long to go to reach that status. They are not without some value as it is likely that the designer was Charles Rennie Mackintosh, who was an architect of some note. He was born in 1868 and died in 1925. Mackintosh was one of the leading figures in the Art Nouveau movement. His architectural design is quite unique and followed the same bold geometrical and straight lines seen in the chairs. He acquired an international reputation in what was then advance design, and was an influence on the 'avant garde' and was much respected in Germany.

Like many great architects, he designed furniture to complement his buildings and these pieces are prized among collectors, although not yet antique. It might also be mentioned that he also designed fabrics and book covers. Mackintosh retired from business in 1923 and devoted his remaining years to watercolour drawing, of which he was so fond. So, your purchase was quite a good one, and the instinct for the unusual has paid off.

My mother has a piece of mahogany furniture which has been in the family for a long time. She calls it a wine cooler. It is octagonal in shape with a band of brass round the lid, top and bottom. It is on a stand, shaped to fit, with four square legs. There are two quite substantial brass handles at the sides and a small matching one for the lid. The wood is beautifully figured and has a deep shine which my mother says is 'elbow grease'. It is quite heavy as it has a metal liner, which I think is lead. Has she got the name right and about how old is it?

An 18th century mahogany wine cooler

The name is quite correct although they are sometimes referred to as pails or tubs. In 17th century Italy, wine was cooled in tubs or silver bowls, and silver bowls were used in England, mostly in the 18th century. The wine coolers of a furnishing design were made to complement the sideboard and it was usual to store them below this or the side table. They were generally made in pairs but it is rare to find a pair together now. Later, the sideboard incorporated a metal lined deep drawer known as a cellarette. The cooler described is a Chippendale example, (legs on the Sheraton design tended to taper). Wine coolers do not all follow the octagonal shape, some are oval and not all have lids; other shapes were used and late Georgian examples were made in sarcophagus style with heavy paw feet. Many handles are lion mask and ring; some are of course without handles. Nearly all coolers are plain and it is exceptional to find one which is decorated with carving.

Your mother's piece (which I hope you will treasure if it eventually comes to you), dates circa 1770. These pieces have taken on a decorative role but can still act as storage for bottles, and suitably placed, serve as an occasional table. I have seen one converted to a sewing box and the liner consequently had been disposed of. Temptation to convert any old piece must be resisted and that cannot be said too often. Conversion completely destroys the antique value.

As a result of seeing a small sideboard advertised, we bought it cheaply as we were looking for a cupboard to fit into a 36 inch wide alcove. We now feel that it is antique but are not sure about that, or the wood from which it is made. Can you offer any information from the following description? There is a shelf at the top held by scroll brackets and this has a fretwork brass rail at the back. There are two drawers with brass handles. The lower part has two doors which do not have glass but brass lattice with a curtain behind. The wood is dark with even darker grain, figured similar to walnut. Are we correct in thinking it antique?

A Regency rosewood chiffonier

Your experience goes to show that pieces of interest can still be discovered and acquired at an advantageous price. Albeit in your case by accident, you now own a Regency 'chiffonier' with a value running into three figures, made in rosewood, a very popular timber used in the early 19th century. The upper shelf with fret brass gallery is an added refinement. Unfortunately in some pieces I have seen, this has been removed. Doors with brass lattice and pleated silk curtains were a typical decorative feature of these pieces, in what might be considered a frivolous age. A chiffonier in this style dates circa 1825 and one should avoid the temptation to remove the brass and curtains to replace them with glass. Later chiffoniers in mahogany and walnut are found with wood panel doors. These small convenient pieces of furniture blend well with the modern and now that you know what you have, it may give you some encouragement to add other antique items to the home. It might be interesting that the name 'rosewood' is a general commercial term given to imported dark wood, obtained from several species of trees whose timber was imported from various countries including the Americas, Burma, Dominica, Jamaica and Australia, with romantic sounding names like Acacia, Glaucescens and Pterocarpus Indicus.

It would be interesting to know the origin and date of a very unusual piece of bedroom furniture, which is thought to be continental. It is made in mahogany with light wood inlay. The centre forms a dressing table with recessed plate glass mirror. Two panel door cupboards are below with a flowering tree inlay. The wing cupboard doors are mirrored with a stylised flowering tree running from top to bottom, supported by bars which seem to be in bronze. We have asked several people about it but have not so far gained any real information. Can you help?

A bedroom combination in Art Nouveau style

The first half of the 19th century produced designers like Pugin whose Gothic-style pieces influenced design for a long period. In the later 19th century, a number of innovations were seen, and furniture design was among them. A movement known as 'the Arts and Crafts' erupted among progressive thinkers like Morris, Ashbee and Mackmurdo, to name but three. They did not want anything to do with commercial standardisation and felt that the Arts and Crafts should combine to produce something quite different in furniture design. Several Guilds were formed in different parts of Britain to encourage the combination of the many skills among architects, designers, leather and metal workers, and cabinet makers. The resulting production gave us the Art Nouveau pieces which now have a place in period history. The result of this combination of different talents really did produce something quite unusual over a quite short period and the impact even caused the commercial makers to start producing along similar lines.

The purists favoured oak rather than mahogany, for they abhorred the thought of 'French polish' preferring to leave wood in its near natural state. The mahogany bedroom combination piece is not continental but English and dates around 1900, perhaps made by a firm like Heal's of London. It shows quality in workmanship of an exacting standard. Art Nouveau furniture has come to the notice of some collectors and I feel that it is well worthwhile to acquire any suitable pieces which can be lived with, while prices are in the region of what can be termed reasonable.

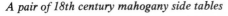

A pair of small mahogany tables have come my way. They have oblong tops and turned single column. The legs are slightly scrolled and square shaped, with small box-like toes without castors. I would be interested to know the period in which they were made. As you can see, the table tops have no corners; were they made in this manner?

A pair of 18th century mahogany side tables

What a pretty pair of side tables, so simple yet effective. The tops were made in this way and are called chamfered angles. These tables were usually placed against the wall, but brought into the room and tea served from them. Without protruding corners there was less likelihood of them being knocked over. They are in the Sheraton manner, and a similar style of tripod feet with small spade toes can be seen on all small tables in the Sheraton designs. Thomas Sheraton, born in the year 1751, became a cabinet maker. Would that he had stayed with that all his working life! He seemed always to be venturing into something different. He ran a bookshop, and became a preacher and wrote about religious subjects, among other things. His publishing venture cost him dearly. With too many irons in the fire, his great gift for wood was dissipated and he lived in constant poverty. He designed as well as made furniture, and his fine work 'The Cabinet Maker and Upholsterers' Drawing Book' which was used as an apprentices' bible, should have made him quite wealthy. Sheraton loved designing and had he concentrated in this field alone, his life might have been much easier, for he died in some poverty in 1804 with little to show for his life's work. We are the more fortunate who have benefited from his talent for design. His work is as much admired as any of the 18th century cabinet makers and designers. Sad for him really, but perhaps he was happy doing all the diverse things he did. He seemed not to desire any material wealth, as he was once heard to say. It is delightful to see these tables still a pair, as they were made and intended to be, around 1780.

We have made a number of alterations to the interior of our house hoping to create an old world atmosphere within the walls of a modern building. We bought old oak beams from a demolition site and these have been placed in position on the ceiling. The fireplaces have been rebuilt in brick with inglenook effect. Although it is artificial it has achieved the object and created the desired illusion of a much earlier period. We have some antique furniture and now have to think of something quite large to occupy a white wall. Can you offer any suggestions?

When converting interiors one has to be careful not to overdo things. The idea of old oak beams seems to have worked out pretty well and is much more satisfactory than artificial creations to simulate them. Old world cottage furniture does add warmth and a cosy feeling, and in the main, is quite comfortable. I would think the white wall is crying out for a dresser and would suggest an 18th ·century Georgian example in oak, but not too dark, with open plate shelves and wing cupboards, frieze drawers and shaped apron, and standing on cabriole supports. An example is illustrated with a pewter display; this would look equally well with, say, blue and white china. Apart from being a

Pewter displayed on an 18th century oak dresser

very elegant piece of furniture it is most useful. Such a piece can usually be found in provincial auction rooms and antique shops. It will hold its value, or better still, increase it and give pleasure over the years to come.

We were wondering if a pair of tub chairs are antique. They are made in mahogany of a reddish colour with inlaid lines of light coloured wood. The backs have rails and open splats, the front arm supports are turned, the seats are padded and covered in tapestry. The front legs are square reducing in thickness and have what is called spade toes. About what date would these chairs have been made?

A pair of Edwardian tub chairs

This type of tub chair formed part of a drawing room suite, although it is fairly rare these days to find one of these suites complete. The design was popular in the Edwardian period. Edwardian design was much influenced by Hepplewhite and Sheraton, and makers and designers who had not succumbed to the style of the Arts and Crafts movement, looked to the 18th century Masters for their ideas. Tub chairs of this order are not yet antique, still a few more years to go to reach the 'magic hundred'. Nice examples will certainly earn their place among the antiques of the future and now is the time to acquire them.

Edwardian furniture, although made in a period of commercial manufacture, shows quality of workmanship, and these pieces with the delicate influence of earlier designers, seem to fit quite well in most surroundings. The square taper legs with spade toes and what is termed satinwood stringing, are reminiscent of Sheraton finery, and chairs of this calibre can be used as occasionals, or with writing and dressing tables, with good effect. Mahogany was imported into this country during the first half of the 18th century and the great use made of it by Thomas Chippendale ensured that it became the most popular wood to be used in cabinet making for a very long time. Mahogany is pinkish brown in colour and takes on a beautiful dark brown hue after long use in the manufactured state. Staining it red is a late Victorian innovation and most Edwardian, and later, mahogany pieces were also treated in this manner. Beech and other woods were also treated in this way and have been termed mahogany on more than one occasion.

In a home furnished entirely with modern furniture, it is difficult to know what sort of antiques will blend in. I would like to add one or two pieces of Victorian furniture which would prove useful as well as decorative. Can any possible suggestions be made?

This is not the first time I have been asked this question and it must be in the minds of many people who would like to live with both old and new. Not all antiques are comfortable to live with, and some of the Victorian antique pieces can be quite bulky and totally unsuitable for present day smaller rooms with low ceilings. The Victorians favoured rosewood, mahogany, oak and walnut and upholstered items, with a fair amount of restrained rococo effect. One piece of furniture which comes to mind and would certainly fit in, is a sofa, settee, chaise longue — call it what you will — of the 1850-60 period. One with a moderately carved mahogany frame, low half back, chair end and cabriole legs in the French style would be pleasing and is one of the prettier types. It will seat three people and is very nice as a day bed. This style looks rather regal in buttoned upholstery, but this is not imperative. A sofa of this description can often be bought in auction, not always with covering in good condition, (which is probably an advantage), for condition affects the price and the colour may be wrong anyway. Some shops offer them already renovated with an undercover, which allows the customer to make his own choice of material. This is the piece I would recommend.

The Victorian 'credenza' also offers a possibility. These were made in Boullework, rosewood, ebonised and mixed woods, but it is walnut which would be best for your purpose. Most credenzas have added ornaments and inlays, some more overpowering than others. The central shelves are enclosed with an attractive panel door, and the end shelves bowed and enclosed by glazed doors. They can act as a drinks cabinet with glasses display, or for china and silver. Both the items described would blend into a modern home, proving both decorative and useful.

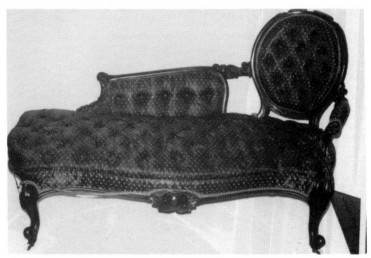

Above, *a Victorian settee with buttoned upholstery.*
Below, *a Victorian credenza*

We have a double burner oil lamp. It has the usual clear glass chimney and opaque shade. The reservoir is vase shape but does not seem to have been made to fit the very nice brass stand which was bought with it. The stand is of the tripod type and looks in the Adam style. Would the stand be earlier than the lamp and is it English?

Lamp and stand

The stand is late 19th century following the Louis XVI style of support seen in the small round top tables known as 'gueridon'. The ormolu examples are sometimes found with a contemporary lamp in Sevres porcelain. The English, late 19th century stands in wrought iron and brass, generally have telescopic columns which incorporate a basket top fitting to hold the reservoir, with a rounded bottom.

The French shades, and many English, were in silk fabric and very attractive. I would think your lamp to be a little later than the stand. If you have a nice 19th century oil lamp and stand, resist the temptation to convert it for electricity. This takes away the value for a collector. A practical oil lamp can be a boon in these modern days. Apart from looking attractive, (and some are very decorative), they can be put into use on those occasions when power supplies are disrupted and an oil lamp will prove much safer and more efficient than a candle.

Is it possible for types of wood used in different periods of furniture making to be defined?

To some degree, a guide can be given, but one cannot lose sight of the fact that most native woods have been used through all periods. In the early periods of Gothic and Tudor, ordinary homes were quite sparsely furnished, mainly comprising a trestle table, benches, coffer chests, and a box or post bed, also a dole cupboard for the storage of food. Oak was the predominant wood, hewn from local forests. It was hard wearing, easy to work, and of course, plentiful. The popularity of oak remained in the Stuart period, and has been used through the centuries, particularly in the country areas.

Walnut came into popularity during the reign of Charles II. Quite new design ideas in decorative furniture developed, no doubt due to the influx of continental craftsmen. This merry monarch has not, I feel, received full credit for his encouragement of the design and arts in Britain. During his reign, walnut was much used and was admirably suitable for the carver's chisel. During the reign of William and Mary the trend in walnut continued and carried into the Queen Anne and early Georgian period. Many of the fine pieces have survived.

When mahogany was imported about 1725, it was very scarce and expensive and it was not until a little later that the general name given to this timber became such a force in English cabinet making. The wood from Central America and the West Indies came from various trees, all belonging to the species Swietenia mahogani; it was not red in colour but brownish pink. After years of use it acquires a beautiful fine brown tint. In the red mahogany pieces of the 19th century the colour was produced by staining. At first, solid mahogany pieces were made but about 1740, the potential of mahogany veneer was realised and it soon superceded the previous walnut figuring.

Great craftsmen designers like Chippendale, Hepplewhite, Sheraton and Adams, used mahogany extensively and it has stood the test of time. The 18th century was, without doubt, the greatest period for cabinet work in general. Other exotic woods were used like kingwood and satinwood and, of course, native beech, ash, elm and fruitwood, but not to the same extent as mahogany. Other woods, pine and satin walnut, for instance, were used from time to time.

The Regency period saw the popularity of rosewood, but mahogany came back strongly with the Victorian period and into the Edwardian era. The mass produced age of the 20th century changed everything. All sorts of carcass wood was used with veneer, much of the pattern photographed or painted under shellac, followed by laminated, chipboard and so on. Only one mahogany and oak period evolved, that of the standard Utility during the Second World War, and one museum in London has thought it worthwhile to preserve items from the period.

Some years ago I bid for a card table at a country house auction; it was eventually knocked down to me at £20. I have to say that my husband was not very pleased about the transaction. However, I have lived with it for many years and have found it a most useful piece of furniture. The wood is dark grained with strips of brass inlaid in the top, which opens up and swivels round. The inside is baized and there is a brass inlay decoration in the frieze. The four legs also have brass rosettes on the scroll end. It was catalogued as antique. About what date was it made?

Above, *an open Regency rosewood card table.*
Below, *same table closed up*

In spite of what your husband thought at the time, he should be quite pleased about your little venture now. It has turned out to be not only useful but a very good investment, and worth over ten times what you originally paid.

This flap over top card table is made with rosewood, a quite popular wood in the Regency period.

The design is typical of the period — early 19th century — when design was influenced by the Greco-Roman. Brass inlaying was only used for a short time and adds to the attractive dark grain wood.

In the 18th century, the gambling habit was in full swing, fortunes were won and lost. Card tables were an essential part of the furnishing in upper class houses, and many beautiful designs appeared in the design books. In the Regency period, it is noticeable that designs for card tables were few and far between; no doubt due to a more pious period when the gambling habit was more frowned upon than approved.

Thankfully, the tables were made and you have a very good example, which has been kept in a pristine condition. The sturdy column, platform and the four generous 'C' scroll feet which terminate in paws and brass castors, makes it quite different from the much lighter looking pieces of the 18th century. It represents a definite period and I am sure you will never regret the day you made your final bid.

Our double chest is in a brownish wood and is quite tall. The top can be lifted off. It is quite a heavy solid piece and well made. The drawers have locks, but we do not have any keys for them. The chest looks old. Can you give some idea of the date?

A mahogany tallboy chest or chest on chest

This is quite a desirable piece of furniture, sometimes referred to as a 'tallboy chest' or as a 'chest on chest'. This is country made and in a straight grain mahogany. The style follows the Chippendale designs. The cornice is of the moulded style with what we call a 'dentil' frieze. All the drawers have cockbead edges which give a nice finish.

The handles are of the relief stamp type rather than a casting, with pierced plates and 'D' grips. They look original. Used as linen chests, tallboys are ideal for that purpose, and only take up the same floor space as a much lower chest of drawers.

Made in two pieces to facilitate easier moving, they are sometimes found with quite substantial brass handles on the sides. The shaped bracket feet are typical on such a piece and are quite strong. All the drawers have individual locks and, more often than not, the keys are missing. New keys can be made if required; it may mean removing the locks and taking them to a locksmith. Date, circa 1780.

We live in an old house with exposed oak beams dating back to 17th century, and have tried to furnish it with pieces which are in keeping. Odd articles have been bought through the years from shops and auctions. One piece, picked up some years ago, always arouses interest and someone always wants to buy it from us. It is a walnut armchair with an unusual, shaped vase back, the arm scrolled, and slightly flatted for the elbow rests; the supports holding these are shaped but very sturdy. The legs are cabriole in shape with quite large knees and pad toes. The rear legs sweep back at least 5 inches, and under the seat there are two iron bars for support. The quadrant blocks at the corners are much larger than normally seen. The seat is 22 inches across and is covered in white hide (by us). There are signs of just a little, but very good, restoration. It would be interesting to know the date this chair was made.

A Queen Anne walnut chair

It would be rare indeed to find a companion chair and I have not seen a similar recorded in books of old furniture. It sounds a very sturdy chair and has stood the test of time. What a distinctive line it has, stamped on it by a fine craftsman in wood, but unfortunately, we can never know who he was. It has a little of the continental influence introduced at the time of William and Mary and was almost certainly made in the reign of Queen Anne. Suffice to say, a very rare chair in near-original condition, and thankfully, restored. It is a possession to be admired and prized and, not for sale, I am sure.

A walnut bureau-cabinet, which is in beautiful condition, is causing some concern since we have been told that our newly-installed central heating could cause it to warp and crack. Can you give any advice?

A Queen Anne walnut bureau-cabinet

This is a superb Queen Anne piece with beautiful walnut figuring, herringbone inlay and crossbanding. The arched door panels in the upper part indicative of the period. The handles and key plates are original and it is nice to see the two candle slides above the bureau top. It looks to be about 37 inches.wide, a size much desired.

The fittings inside these pieces are always made with the same loving care as the outside.

It is interesting to note the wide gap between the slope fall and the first drawers. This indicates a well fitment, and these pieces usually have one or more secret compartments, which are easy to find in later pieces, but not so simple in the earlier ones.

Atmospheric conditions created by central heating can prove harmful to prime pieces of old furniture. The craftsman certainly could not have anticipated such conditions. Some quite devastating damage can occur, particularly in the side timbers where there is a wider expanse of wood. I have seen pieces which have opened up to quite a degree.

In rooms which contain several old pieces, the humidifier is the ideal piece of equipment. There are also specially designed troughs to hang on radiators. These evaporate very quickly and require regular topping up.

It has always been my advice to keep pot-plants in rooms containing the precious furniture. A wilting plant is its own reminder that water is required. Vases of flowers can also help to keep humidity constant. It is unwise to place antique furniture close to a radiator for proximity temperature can be quite high and will dry out wood very quickly.

Periodical examination should be carried out during the times of the year when temperatures are considerably raised to dry heat, to make sure that nothing is going amiss.

So long as the moisture content in a room is adequate, using one or more of the above mentioned precautions, your inheritance will be preserved.

Can you advise me what to do with an antique chest which is infected with woodworm. I have been told that I should burn the piece as it will spread to my other furniture. Would this be the best thing to do?

It is regrettable that many have acted on the advice you have been given, and consequently many quite valuable items of antiquity have been lost. Your chest can, and should be, preserved. The furniture beetle (Anobium Punctatum) commonly known as woodworm has, it seems, always been with us. It is a flying insect about one eighth of an inch long and brown in colour. The female beetle deposits between twenty and sixty eggs in an available crevice in the wood. After a period of two weeks, small white grubs with brown heads develop. Like all babies, they are hungry, and soon start to eat their way into the wood, leaving tunnels in their wake. This is what weakens the timber.

The period the pests stay in the wood varies. In most home conditions it is two years, but it has been known to stay for up to twenty years where the atmosphere is cool. Eventually the grubs eat their way to lie just below the surface, where they remain for the pupation period of about two weeks. In this situation the grubs turn into beetles and eat their way out, leaving the tell-tale hole and often traces of fine dust. The females mate quite quickly after emerging and the whole cycle begins again.

Most woods are vulnerable to attack, although I have never seen it in ebony or Chinese hardwood. Softwoods are the more easily weakened. Bamboo and plywood seem very susceptible. Floor and roof timbers are also subject to infestation and in these areas often goes undiscovered for years, until a collapsing timber manifests that something is wrong. Semi-damp conditions are favoured and bathroom floors can be infected. The beetles usually come to maturity in late spring and summer. They are not easily seen, and barely move when not flying.

A minute scattering of fine dust near furniture should be investigated; if there is infection the small emersion holes, which resemble those made by a dart, will be found somewhere, mainly underneath or at the back. Glued blocks used in angle fixing are often soft wood and can be a source of the trouble. Treatment is a must. There are special fluids on the market and you can treat furnishings yourself, following the directions carefully. There are also polishes that act as a deterrent. I would advise two treatments at weekly intervals, then another the following year as a precaution. Once treatment is completed, fill the exit holes with wax polish, using your finger. I find tan shoe polish quite good for this purpose. You may ask, why bother to fill the holes? The answer is, that it allows you to spot any newly made holes and know that further treatment is necessary. Structural woodwork is a different matter and best left to the professional firms, who can treat and replace timber where necessary.

I would certainly never destory an antique piece because of woodworm infection. Old wood is strong wood, and it is rarely weakened sufficiently to require major repair.

Some months ago we inherited a table which is rectangular when closed, but opens up to form a square top with a green baize cover. The wood has a dark grain with lighter inlaid strips. It has four supports with a base and four shaped legs with castors. What period is the table, and does it have any particular value?

The table is in rosewood with satinwood stringing. The period is Regency, about 1818. This is a purpose-made card table, the flap over top swivels to rest securely on the frame. The turned pillar supports terminating on the X platform are pleasing, the shaped sabre form legs, with castor toes, are a feature of the period. These quite pretty tables were an essential part of both Georgian and later Victorian drawing rooms. When not being used for games, they were closed and placed against a wall to act as side tables.

These card tables still have their use and are a decorative attraction in present day homes; they are becoming rare on the market and the chance to acquire one should not be missed. You have inherited a reasonably valuable piece, which can be prized and admired.

4 Silver

Should I specialise in silver, and what would be the best period?

A pair of pierced Georgian silver coasters

Silver does make a good but more expensive collection; the Georgian period gives great scope covering a long period from 1714 to 1830. Tea sets, mugs, sauceboats and similar things will be rather expensive. The less costly flat ware is quite interesting and provides numerous opportunities. Start with salt scoops, tea spoons, dessert and table spoons, forks and sauce ladles, because these are not too difficult to find singly and in pairs, and it is possible to make up a set of six in a fairly short time. Table spoons and forks seem the more plentiful, dessert spoons are rarer. Do not be deterred by crests on flatware; most families in the past identified their silver in this way. It can be an added attraction for many of the armorials can be traced. Unlike most other antiques, silver is much easier to date and often even the maker can be identified.

Moving on from the Georgian period, there is the short period of William IV followed by the long Victorian reign; this silver continues to bear the monarch's head in the mark and is very attractive.

Can you give information about the age of a silver frame cruet stand which has quite large shell feet and contains two cut glass bottles and three casters; the bottles have what looks like silver tops but are not marked. The casters are baluster in shape with rope borders, the tops finely worked and pierced. The marks on the base of the frame are not in line, but spread out and show a capital 'Q', a figure similar to that of Britannia, the letters W.C. and a harp. I understand that this is an Irish mark and one of my great grandparents came from there.

A Georgian cruet

The stand sounds to be complete with original condiments. Cruet stands were made in this style in both England and Ireland in the Georgian period. They are often referred to as 'Warwick' and there are several stories about the name. The most feasible is a demand by the Earl to have his condiments kept together, and a stand was made to hold them all. Silver condiment pieces were always fairly elaborate, one of the most beautiful and rare pieces being the English standing salt dated 1589 in possession of the Goldsmiths Company. The collection of this great institution is worth viewing if the opportunity arises. In the marks on Dublin plate the figure represents Hibernia, the name given to Ireland by Latin writers, who probably took it from Aristotle's reference to the island which he spoke of as 'Irene'. The capital Q represents the year 1764 and W.C. the registered mark of goldsmith William Currie.

The large scallop shell feet on these stands are characteristic as is the cartouche which often bears an armorial or monogram. Tops on the glass bottles were not usually marked, but marks on casters should be of the same date as the frame, to ensure that they have not been changed or the frame made up. For some years, particularly at the latter end of the 19th century and the early years of this century, frames were not popular and many were confined to the melting pot. When Britain went off the gold standard in 1930 great quantities of gold and silver articles were melted down; people were encouraged by the government to sell their valuables for scrap. Casters seemed to have been more successful survivors and many seen now were probably part of a frame set. A complete matched set in a stand of 18th or 19th century date is very collectable now in silver or plate.

Before the Second World War, I bought a box of what was described as 'sundries' at an auction for a few shillings. It contained a quantity of odds and ends, mostly damaged. Among them was a small round teapot, plain except for a little decoration at the top; it did not have a handle but was otherwise in good condition. When cleaned up, it looked quite attractive. Eventually it was taken to a jeweller who put a new handle on it. At the time he said it was an antique. It has remained in a china cabinet all these years — actually it's too small to be used. We would now like to sell it. The marks on it are a leopard's head wearing a crown, a lion, a small letter 'd' in a shield and the letters IH in capitals with a small crown on top. Where would be the best place to take it?

An 18th century bullet teapot

You have what is known as a globular or bullet teapot. These started to appear round the 1720's. They were diminutive which emphasizes the precious quality of the tea leaf in those days. They were generally plain, some having a little decoration as the rococo influence crept in. Those found with heavy embossing were given this treatment at a later date. The Victorians had quite a mania for embossing earlier, quite plain pieces of silver, thereby ruining the aesthetic value. Lids on these little pots were sometimes hinged and it is noticeable that lids were quite small. The handles, usually in ebony, occasionally in ivory, varied slightly from pot to pot. The replacement handle is probably of ebonised wood and is in keeping, and is not having too much of a detrimental effect on the value.

From the marks you have described, this piece dates 1739 and hallmarked at the London Assay Office. The letters IH are the maker's initials. In silver marks the I represents J. The mark is recorded as that of John Harwood, who enered the Company of Goldsmiths in 1734. As you say, the pot is not large enough for general use today, but it is a delightful piece to have and most collectors of antique silver would be interested in it.

If you feel you must part with it, than a good auction room is probably the best means of selling. There are quite a number who hold specialist sales. They are not difficult to find; newspapers and specialist magazines carry advertisements from these auction rooms. The auctioneer will advise you about the reserve figure which should be placed on an item. This protects you as the lot will not be sold unless it reaches that figure. Your teapot will, without doubt, find a good home where it will be cared for and preserved for posterity.

We have a small piece of silver which we think was a bell, but the clapper is missing. It is shaped like a fox head. There is a lion silver mark on the rim, together with a crowned leopard, a man's face, a capital letter H and AB and GB. Should we have a new clapper fitted?

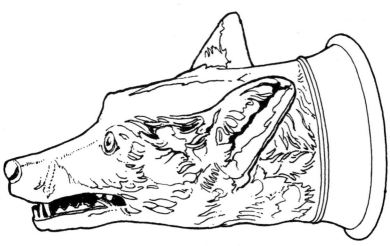

A Georgian stirrup cup

It is as well that your enthusiasm for a bell has not caused you to go ahead with the addition, which would have probably ruined the value of what is quite a rare item. You have an antique 'stirrup cup'. The dictionary defines it as 'a parting cup on horseback'. These cups were filled with hot punch or brandy and handed to the riders at the start of the hunt. Some were personalised with a coat of arms, or a monogram. The drink was quaffed and the cup returned. The custom still continues.

The piece is circa 1804, hallmarked in London. The initials are those of Alice and George Burrows, entered at the Goldsmiths Company in 1802. It was not unusual in those days to find husband

and wife teams and sometimes relationships were more widely stretched, as in the well-known Bateman family.

Stirrup cups in the form of a foxhead were made from mid-18th century and well into the 19th century. The early examples show a less natural and more elongated head. Stirrup cups are easily faked by soldering a band bearing an old mark on to a more recently cast foxhead. Fortunately, we do not find too much faking with silver, but it has happened. Sometimes at an auction you may see a dealer breath on a piece of silver. He is looking for a well-disguised repair or insert.

We have a tankard which has been in our family for many years and must be over a hundred years old. The tankard is in perfect condition, with a dome topped hinged lid with a shaped thumbpiece. The handle is in the shape of a letter 'S' with a heart at the base. It has marks which are a leopard head with a crown, a lion, a capital letter 'O' and two old English letters TM. It would be interesting to know who made it and when?

A Georgian covered tankard

Silver has always been one of my favourites. So many lovely pieces have been made over the centuries. The durability and precious nature of the metal is the reason why so much has survived. Most pieces were made for practical use and are still as good today as they were new. Tankards were very popular items and goodness knows how many were made since the days of the leather jack which was used for drinking. Tankards are still with us and often used as presentation items today. You are fortunate with yours, for its high dome cover has not been tampered with, or improved as it was mistakenly thought, by chasing, embossing or altering at a later date. Some 18th century tankards can be found with added pouring lips, an obvious alteration.

Your piece is a fine example of the George II period. The date letter 'O' indicates that it was Assayed 1749-50 year. (Date letters change in the month of May, not at the beginning of the year, therefore the same alphabetical letter serves over parts of two years). The goldsmiths were, and still are, governed by many statutes and were required to register their mark. In the early centuries these were devices. About the middle of the 16th century, initials as well as devices appeared or combination of both. Later, just initials were used with sometimes the occasional small device added. The initials, or mark, on your tankard, are those registered by Thomas Mann in 1736. The statutes have proved most helpful to collectors of silver for they enable accurate dating.

Sometimes, marks have been rubbed away by harsh cleaning. It is prudent to protect marks when cleaning by covering with the finger or thumb to prevent rubbing, it is sufficient just to rub over the mark with the ball of the thumb. It is interesting that this part of the hand has been used by silver polishers over many years and there is a saying 'red as a butler's thumb' indicating the stain left by silver cleaning rouge.

Silver, and plate for that matter, requires careful consideration, only the softest of cleaners and clothes should be used. I prefer sifted whiting mixed to a paste with methylated spirit, and applied with a piece of cotton wool. Alternatively rouge and chamois leather can be used. It might be a bit more difficult, but worthwhile on results and is free of the rather unpleasant clinging odour left by some commercial silver cleaners.

There has been some argument about a punch ladle we have in our small collection of silver items. Because of its colour and condition we think it is silver. Other opinions (not experts, I might add) differ, and they think it is plate, because it does not have the recognised marks. It is oval in shape with a lip for pouring. The handle is a twisted dark brown material, not wood, and has a silver end point. There is some kind of mark which looks like an elephant, a letter A and H & Co. From what I have described, can you define if it is silver?

This is not the first time that confusion has arisen over silver marks. Quite a number of provincial marks cause confusion among laymen. Many towns marked their silversmiths' work in different ways and did not include the lion. Many statutes were created in respect to silver. One issued in 1690, and which caused a lot of fuss, was one

A Georgian punch ladle with a whalebone handle

which decreed that all silver had to be taken to London for Assay. Can you imagine the impossibility of it in the days of horse transport, to say nothing about footpads and highwaymen! The situation lasted five or six years before Provincial Offices were re-established at places like Norwich, Newcastle, Chester, Exeter and York. None of these exist today. Chester Provincial Assay offices was the last to close in this century. In the smaller areas where goldsmiths worked, the towns were recognised by their own special mark which are numerous but can be identified with a little reading. These small town marks have undoubtedly caused many pieces of silver to be mistaken for plate.

The mark similar to that which you describe on your ladle was used at Perth in Scotland by Hamilton and Company towards the end of the 18th century, which dates the piece circa 1790. The handle is of whalebone and this is frequently seen on Georgian toddy ladles because it acts as a heat insulator.

Punch ladles are often found without marks and sometimes the bowls were fashioned from a beaten silver coin or had a coin insert, (the date on the coin not necessarily the date the piece was made). The use of coinage and non-marking leads one to believe that these small pieces were a goldsmiths sideline. Incidentally, Hamilton and Company established a business in Calcutta early in the 19th century and used a similar mark.

Punch ladles offer an interesting variation to the collector, for they can be found in a number of different designs.

We have a rather nice Georgian three-piece tea set, and we have often wondered who made it. All the pieces are perfectly plain in, what I think is called, boat shape. The set is in prime condition. The teapot has a black handle and knob on the lid, and stands on small ball feet. The mark consists of a leopard's face with a crown, capital letter T, the monarch's head, and the letters R.E. over EB. Can you offer a suggestion who the maker might be?

A Georgian three-piece tea set

This is a very nice, plain set of the desirable oblong form. The marks are intact and readable, something not always found on these plain sets, which were made for everyday use. (We often lose sight of this fact when we see them in a collector's cabinet.)

Tea has been responsible for bringing us a legacy of beautiful pieces of silver concerned in its preparation. First heard of in this country about the middle of the 17th century, referred to as 'tay or tee', from the Chinese 'tcha'.

It is pleasant to use an antique service now and again and prepare the tea in the same careful way of long ago, warming the pot and using a stirring spoon. I do not think that Rebecca Eames or Edward Barnard will mind if you enjoy the use of their tea set. They sat beating away on your pot in 1814 and registered their mark, which appears on your set, in 1808.

We have a sugar bowl which is quite plain apart from a fleur de lis crest on the side. It is 6 inches wide and the bowl is gilt on the inside. It stands on a pedestal foot and has reeded edges and handle. The marks are a crowned leopard's head, monarch's head, a capital letter 'S' and the initials H.G. Can you say what date it was made?

The sugar bowl is part of a late Georgian service in a plain, classical boat shape.

A sugar bowl made in 1813

Early 18th century sugar bowls were hemispherical, and usually fitted with covers that had a rather large ring handle, which when not being used for covering the bowl, could be inverted and used as an additional dish. Sugar was refined in England from about the 1650's. Loaf sugar was made in much larger moulds than the cubes we know today and was cut into smaller pieces with sugar nippers (a scissor-like implement with axe-like cutting blades). Sugar tongs evolved early 18th century and early examples had a scissor action and scallop shell bowls, or with long blades similar to the beak of a stork. Tongs of the more familiar type were used after mid-century.

This sugar bowl is pleasing in shape and bears a family crest; most families marked their silver in this manner. It dates 1813 and was possibly made by Henry Greene.

We have a pair of candlesticks, quite heavy for their size. They appear to be cast and quite rough under the bases. The edges and stems are fluted, the stems resemble a stone garden urn in shape. They do not have the removable tops, presumably these have been lost. The marks are stamped under the bases but are not very clear to read. There is definitely a crowned leopard head, one letter looks like an old English B, a lion and two old English letters most difficult to define, one looks to be a C, about the other we are not sure. There seems to be a small star over the top. The candlesticks stand 6 inches high. Is it possible to date them?

It does sound as if you have a fairly valuable pair of cast silver candlesticks. This style was made from the end of the 17th century. They were cast in several pieces by the method introduced by the Huguenots who fled from persecution on the Continent and settled

An 18th century candlestick

here. These people brought great skills with them and we have much to thank them for. Paul De Lamerie, a fine goldsmith, was among them. The marks on cast candlesticks are never very clear because, being struck on a very rough surface, they tend to spread. The sconces have not been lost for they were never there. If they are found with sconces, these are usually later additions.

Cast silver candlesticks were made from about 1690. The style started to change about 1765 and we see more of the rolled sheet silver work with weighted bases. Silver design was often dictated by a tax-per-ounce-levy to meet the needs of the Sovereign.

The marks suggest that this pair, which were probably a set of four, were made in 1757 and by William Cafe, who seems to have made more candlesticks than most. He registered his initials with a mullet over them in that year. Like many other silver antiques, candlesticks offer a good range for the collector and have a grace of line, which cannot fail to please.

It would be interesting to know when chamber candlesticks were first used. We have a plain reed-edged example, complete with cap. The hallmarks show a crowned leopard's head, a lion, capital I, and initials J.E. When did this type of candlestick come into use?

The chamber candlestick, so called because it was intended to light one to bed, came into use in the 17th century. The earlier sticks, which are rare, (Queen Anne examples are very hard to find), had a much deeper saucer with pan-like handles. Some of the columns had cut-aways to facilitate easy removal of the candle stump. In the 18th century handles became shorter and finally developed into a scroll type about 1740. 18th century pieces were fairly plain, but in the 19th

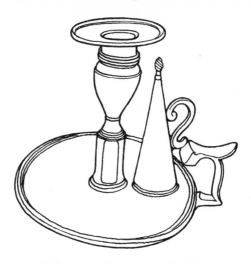

A Georgian chamber candlestick

century, with its passion for added decoration, they became more ornate. Some later examples became taller and more vase-like. The conical extinguishers which are essential for trapping the candle gas, should bear the same date mark as the base. This example has a cut-away, intended to house a pair of snuffers and is seen in many, but not all, chambersticks of later date. The snuffers usually have steel blades with silver handles, it might give you some interest to seek out a pair to go with the stick. This piece, with removable sconce, dates 1805 and the initials are those registered by John Emes.

Having bought a spirit stand and entreé dish which was catalogued as plate, we find that the stand has a mark inside the leg which indicates that it is silver. The marks are a leopard's head, a lion, old English small 'e', monarch's head and J.A. The lamp and dish are unmarked. Would they also be silver as they came in one lot?

The dish stand is certainly silver of 1860 date and the initials are those of Joseph Angel, a London goldsmith. There has been a mix-up somewhere along the line, for the lamp and dish are no doubt plated by the electro method which evolved in Britain in 1840, as a result of work by Thomas Spencer of Liverpool who set up the first plating business about that time. The process was partly discovered in experiments by Volta and Galvani, and Jacobi of St. Petersburg was working on it at about the same time as Spencer, so Britain cannot claim full credit. However, the process which was much cheaper,

An entrée dish on a stand with a spirit lamp underneath

certainly stopped the production of Sheffield plate. Your pieces have come together by mistake and probably someone, somewhere, has a Victorian dish and lamp with a plated stand. It is not unusual for things to get mixed up, particularly during family division. I have seen plenty of examples with Georgian bases and Victorian lids and vice versa. You have benefited buying the lot as plate and perhaps one day you may come across a Victorian lamp and entreé dish.

When we bought an antique silver tankard from a shop, the ticket described it as an early George III baluster tankard, not in original condition. It has a domed top, with open lifting piece, the handle is 'S' shape with a heart end, and it is embossed with scroll leaves and flowers. We examined it very carefully but could not find evidence of repair. The mark does not include the monarch's head. It looked so nice and we bought it at what we thought was a very reasonable price. Can you explain what might have been wrong with it?

If you had given me full information about the hallmark I could have dated it for you. It sounds like a piece from the early 1760's. The King's head is a duty paid mark and was not used in that period although duty was payable. The mark was used from 1784 until 1890 in England and Scotland. Monarchs' heads have appeared on later silver but these are for commemorative purposes.

The wording on the ticket was not concerned with repair but with decoration, which your dealer recognised as being added at a later

An embossed Georgian tankard

date. It is not uncommon to find later decoration, particularly in the 19th century. Attempts have been made to restore silver to its original condition, but is generally not successful due to the stretching of the silver body caused by the embossing. Later embossing affects values and the price asked is usually substantially lower than that of an original plain piece of silver. This tankard has not been too overdone, (many are completely covered using every available space).

You have found a dealer who is knowledgeable and fair and can safely place yourself in his hands for future purchases.

Does the fact that a piece of silver has an engraved presentation inscription affect the value? We have an oval dessert bowl which has 'C' scroll and waved edge. The decoration is extensive with embossed roses, leaves and scrollwork and dot punched all over between the decoration. The base of the bowl is line and dot punched in the shape of a scallop shell and stands on four hoof feet. The inscription is dated 1894. The hallmark is very difficult to find; it is E and Co with lion, leopard's head and a capital 'S'. We are told it weighs 30 ounces. The bowl is gilded inside.

We often find that some presentation pieces are earlier than the inscribed date; however this one is contemporary. It sounds quite ornate and, as you say, marks on pieces with extensive embossing are difficult to find. This problem is found with things like dressing mirrors. I would think they are an an Assay Office nightmare, for indiscriminate mark punching could spoil the look of a piece!

Some inscriptions can affect a value, depending on the extent and execution. In many cases the silver is thick enough to allow removal. It is as well to feel and compare thickness of possible inscription sites when making a purchase. (I have seen many pieces of table flatware which show evidence of monogram removal.) Even with the inscription, this is quite a nice dessert bowl. You could explore the possibility of removal but, better still, try and trace the recipient, and you might discover a bit of history.

Among my small collection of snuff boxes there is a very small one shaped like a book. It is about 1 inch long. It is hallmarked with an anchor, old English 'm', lion, monarch's head and initials T & P. The lid opens to reveal an inner cover which is beautifully saw-pierced and inside of the box is gilt. When were snuff boxes made as small as this? Was the grill cover used to sprinkle snuff on to the back of the hand?

What you have described is not a snuff box but a 'vinaigrette'. These followed on from the earlier pomander. Originally, a small sponge was placed below the grill and soaked with aromatic vinegar. (Like the pomander, it was a necessary personal piece in the days before the hygienic facilities of today!) Vinaigrettes are found in several shapes, some a little exotic, formed like a fish, or small enough to be fitted into a ring or the top of a walking stick. Others come in circular form with a chain ring like a watch. In all, quite a range. This example is William IV and dates 1835, made by the Birmingham goldsmiths John Taylor and John Perry.

Vinaigrettes seemed to go out of fashion after the middle of the 19th century, and are now quite sought after collectors' pieces. Nathaniel Mills and Gervaise Wheeler seem to be the most highly prized makers in this field.

A silver object on wheels, in the form of a galleon with sails, guns and sailors, has always intrigued me. I have never heard it referred to as other than a Continental 'Nef'. What was this piece used for and how did it get such a name?

These are quite intriguing objects and seem to turn up from time to time, made in silver, and Continental, but not confined to one particular country. The name 'Nef', which is also given to a mill on a boat, simply means 'ship' and these pieces always take this form. They are quite a work of art, requiring a tremendous amount of goldsmiths' skill. The Nef seems to go back into mediaeval times and there must

A Nef or ship from Europe

be some mythological influence somewhere along the line. Early pieces were usually made in gold, later in silver gilt, then silver. They seemed to have been used for holding rare spices at the banquet tables of kings and nobles and among the Papal hierarchy. They were also made in goblet form and seemed to have been used in ceremonies such as coronations and similar affairs. A Nef made at Nuremburg in the 17th century in the form of a goblet has similar decoration to that always found, (i.e. repoussé work), depicting waves and fish, with figures on deck and in the rigging. Dolphins frequently figure in them and guns are often seen on deck. They all have similar elaborate decoration. The tops complete with deck can be lifted off, forming a cover for the spicy sweetmeat contents. Wheels allow them to be coasted round the table. Attractive in a rather unusual way, but a problem to clean, therefore best seen in a cabinet. More a sculpture than a condiment set.

If you are a beginner with under £3000 to spend, it is difficult to know exactly what to collect, particularly when one is thinking of investment as well as having nice things to live with. Would you consider that we are thinking along the correct lines by concentrating on antique silver? What would be your comments on the following:—A coffee pot, marked with an old English small 'h', leopard's head, date letter and initials G.A. A tankard with domed cover, marked with crowned leopard's head, date letter capital 'S'. A spirit kettle and stand, marked crowned leopard's head, date letter small 'r'. A pair of sauce-boats, with crowned leopard's head, monarch's head, date letter capital 'A' and initials H.C. Would pieces like these be considered a sound basis for a collection?

From left, *Victorian coffee pot, George II tankard, 18th century spirit kettle, sauceboats dated 1796*

Silver is an excellent choice for anyone with a dual purpose in mind. It is durable, always looks attractive if properly tended, and can be easily transported. There is not much to be said against silver and what better to hand on to one's children than a good collection of silver.

The coffee pot is Victorian, dating 1864, the letters G.A. being the registered mark of George Angell, a London goldsmith, the possible maker of the piece. The George II tankard of plain cylindrical form, dates 1733. These were very popular during the period and we are fortunate that quite large numbers have survived. The spirit kettle is more of a rarity and dating 1753 and probably weighs in the region of sixty ounces, quite a volume of precious metal apart from the workmanship. It is always nice to have such a piece in a collection. The sauceboats always look beautiful, they have a grace of line which one can only admire. Dated 1796 with the registered, or entered mark as it is termed, of Henry Chawner, a quite well-known London goldsmith.

A collection such as this still leaves you with sufficient funds for perhaps some flatware. Sauce ladles can be found in pairs and spoons and forks from George III period can still be frequently found in provincial salerooms. It is advisable to make some study of the subject and there are a number of reference works available. Pocket size books for date reference can be bought quite cheaply and are always handy on your expeditions.

Mixed bundles of flatware are often offered at auction and are always worth examining. I started off with odd lots myself and gradually swopped around over the years to acquire place settings for six, (of the same date), although I must admit I have not yet succeeded in obtaining all the same makers. There is a lot of pleasure in doing it this way and no reason why one should not buy odd pieces to start. Silver, like shares, has its up and down periods, and it pays to keep an eye on the market. No one knows what silver will be worth in years to come, but it is fairly certain that it will not be worth less than it is today.

I remember that many years ago, buyers used to reckon one pound an ounce for the bulk of antique silver and, at auction, items were often sold by the ounce. That situation has changed, but if you know the weight, (and auctioneers often make a note in the catalogue for the heavier pieces), you may be able to work out your own system for buying and determine in your own mind how much per ounce you are prepared to pay. If you take note you will often see trade buyers on view day, weighing pieces on their hold up 'troy' scales. The trade have to be keen and cannot afford to get carried away if they want to stay in business.

Is there an easy method which could be used by the smaller collector for dating silver periods?

There are, of course, a vast number of different marks on silver made in the British Isles. To display them would take up the whole of this book. Items bought at auction and in shops are usually dated as this stimulates the sale. It is the odd chance which comes your way, then it is necessary to know a little about the subject in order to take advantage of a possible good buy.

There are quite a number of Provincial Assay Offices which no longer operate. These are too numerous and varied to allow their marks to be quickly learned. The main Offices where most of the antique silver was marked are: London, Birmingham, Sheffield, Chester, Edinburgh, Glasgow, Dublin. You will see evidence of these quite often.

Under a Statute of Edward I, the marking of silver became law, and various statutes have been in force through the ages. Even today, silver cannot be offered for sale as such unless it is properly marked according to the law.

To avoid confusion, it would be best to commence with the date 1784 when the duty mark appeared. George III raised many taxes and silver was taxed by weight. The evidence of the tax paid was indicated by the addition of the monarch's head to the Assay or Hallmark, as it has come to be termed. So we have our first easy guide. Hallmarks also show a leopard's head, as it is generally called, although I have always felt that this is really a lion's head, the name leopard arising from the translation of the Norman French word for lion. From the early days of hallmarks, the leopard was shown with a crown and this continued until 1821. A fairly simple rule to remember is that where the leopard is crowned and the monarch's head is seen on a piece of English silver, the article is George III period. From 1821 the King's head still appeared with leopard uncrowned and continued until the end of Queen Victoria's reign when the duty was lifted. All silver marked with the monarch's head is collectable, including King George V Jubilee, which shows both King and Queen, this being the only period when this has happened.

Assay Offices outside London had their own mark of identification. Birmingham, the anchor; Sheffield, the crown; Chester (now closed), three wheatsheaves with a sword; Edinburgh, three-turret castle and thistle; Glasgow, tree, fish and bell; Dublin, harp and figure representing Hibernia (similar to Britannia). It is interesting that the monarch's head did not appear on Dublin marked silver until 1806. The Hibernia device had been used to indicate duty paid, or so it was said. There seems to have been considerable evasion of duty, due to the fact that Commissions of Revenue had omitted to make Hibernia an official mark. The famous Keating trial brought things to a head and the matter was corrected by statute.

Silver collectors have some advantage over others because pieces are marked with letters which indicate the date and with makers' initials. By using one of many books on marks, a piece can be accurately dated and often the name of the maker discovered. As all the Assay Offices used a different cycle of date lettering, it would be too confusing to mention them here at any length. A rough guide to London letter dating may be of some assistance:—1784 to 1795, small Roman letters; 1796 to 1815, Roman capitals; 1816 to 1835, Roman small letters; 1836 to 1855, black letter capitals (old English style); 1856 to 1875, black small letters; 1876 to 1895, Roman capitals.

It should now be recognised how useful the books of specialised reference can be when it comes to marks on silver.

5 Silver Plate

Is it possible that a pair of coasters in our possession are old Sheffield plate? They are 6 inches in diameter, with turned mahogany bases and with a silver spot in the centre. There is some copper showing through in places. The edge is roped and the body fluted.

A pair of Sheffield coasters

These are Sheffield plate coasters, early 19th century, (circa 1810), and seem to suffer the not unusual complaint of copper showing through. This is the result of wear and constant cleaning, the process being known as 'bleeding'. Coasters or decanter stands were used to protect polished surfaces from drip stain. They were made in many decorative forms, plain, saw-pierced and fluted, like your own. Early examples were fairly shallow. Those made in the late 18th and early 19th century seem to have become deeper. Edges were roped, gadrooned, beaded, or turned over, and for a very good reason.

Sheffield plate was manufactured by the process of fusing a sheet of copper between two sheets of silver, and the copper was visible at the edges, hence the added decoration which served to hide the join. The ware is not really plated as we have come to understand the word.

Any useful article made in silver could also be made in Sheffield plate — teapots, creamers, sugar bowls, tea caddies were popular pieces. Plate was much cheaper than silver, and the heavy taxes levied on the metal by George III's statutes, did much to expand the use of Sheffield plate. At the beginning of the 19th century a tax of one shilling and sixpence was levied on every ounce of silver — and this was no mean sum in those days.

Decanter stands can be quite decorative and although many are no longer used for their original purpose, they can serve as occasional dishes for nuts and sweets. It is well worth collecting a pair or two made in Sheffield plate. There are quite a number of designs to choose from.

We have a rather peculiar article which has caused quite a deal of speculation as to its function. It looks like silver but is not hallmarked. The frame is oval in shape and stands on a pedestal foot. There is a bar with a turnkey end running from side to side across the centre, to which a fine chain is attached. There is also a small ball with a hole in it soldered to the side. It has a small burner nozzle at the top of the frame. It is 4½ inches high. Can you say what it is?

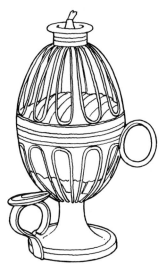

A wax jack or taper holder

From what you have described, this is without doubt a wax jack, otherwise known as a taper holder. The centre key bar was passed through the roll of soft wax taper and threaded into the burner. When lit, the taper burns like a candle, a slight turn of the key fed more taper as it burned. Some are found in silver with hallmarks. This example is Sheffield plate dated circa 1800. It was a very necessary piece of equipment in the days when correspondence was sealed with wax, and would also have been used in a lawyer's office for document seals.

In the 1800's, most people of note had their own personal seal in the form of a ring, fob, or a desk piece with a decorative handle of amethyst, amber, ivory, etc. The small piece at the side would have held a small conical cap, similar to those on chamber sticks. When putting out the flame, these caps trap the wax gas, which gives off that unpleasant smell we have all experienced. Soft wax tapers are difficult if not impossible to obtain, so for the look of the piece you could warm a long taper and attach this carefully.

We have what is known as a wine cooler. It has two handles and the edges are decorated with dragoon work. It looks like silver but there are no hallmarks. When tested with a 'siltest' pencil, it did not show a negative reaction. Could the piece be silver although it is not marked?

An 18th century wine cooler

When making a test for silver it is not sufficient to test the surface. One has to get below by filing or grooving, choosing a place, (as is the practice at the Assay offices), where it will not be noticed. The same also applies to gold. I am sure that when you get below the surface of this wine cooler you will find copper. Do not despair about this, for a piece of old Sheffield plate can have quite a value, for it is getting to be a fairly rare commodity. Plate was made only over about a 100-year period. The process consisted of fusing silver to copper and was discovered by Thomas Bolsover of Sheffield in 1743, some say by accident. Nevertheless, he was able to manufacture small items, mostly boxes, which resembled silver boxes of the period. Another Sheffield man, Joseph Hancock, realised the potential and further improvements allowed silver to be fused on both sides of the copper. No solder was used in the process, it was the controlled temperature, hammering, rubbing, and rolling which fused the metal and produced sheet material with which to work. First called copper rolled plate, it seemed to acquire the name of Sheffield plate about the year 1770. By the late 18th century there was a flourishing trade in Sheffield, for the plate enabled everything that was normally made in silver to be copied and thus the silver tax was avoided. Marks did not seem to appear on early Sheffield plate. No doubt the goldsmiths, (whose trade it could not help but affect), used their influence to prevent any marks which might resemble silver. In 1784 a statute allowed the marking of the plate with a maker's device and sometimes a name also, which had to be registered at the Sheffield Assay Office. Not all makers bothered to use the statute and did not register.

There are quite a large number of recorded firms and marks, some registered 1784-85 were J. Parsons and Co., (Crossed Keys), Nathaniel Smith, (a hand), Dixon and Co., (a star), Robert Cadmam, (a bell), Matthew Boulton, (a sun). Quite a number registered in the 19th century, one of the better known being the Crossed Arrows of T. & J. Creswick.

A piece of Sheffield plate in good condition is as prized as silver among collectors. Plate requires care in preservation and harsh cleaning can be ruinous. Sheffield plate has a different appearance to the more modern electro plate, and, with a little experience, can be recognised. Your specimen is a good example and probably dates late 18th century.

We have a cream jug made in silver pattern. It looks pewter but is marked Britannia metal. Can you explain what this metal is?

Britannia metal came on the scene very late 18th century. It is a pewter form with a copper content but is much harder than normal pewter and has a ringing tone when struck. This metal seems to have been neglected in the collecting field and so far there has not been any great interest in it. It was also marketed under various trade names, like 'Argentine plate' and 'Queen's metal'. The consistency of the metal allows it to be highly polished like silver, but once it is allowed to become really dull, it is impossible to revive its former sheen. Many useful wares were made from the early 19th century using the die stamping and moulding process, which allowed a mass production. Both John Vickers and John Dixon of Sheffield were concerned in manufacture at the beginning of the 19th century, and their names can be found on some pieces. Among other makers were Holdsworth, Ashberry, Broadhead and Atkins. Early pieces are plain and after about 1842 engraved and decorated by the block and roller method. Quite a lot of later pieces were silver plated, but wear and cleaning removed it fairly quickly. These pieces are identified by the letters E.P.B.M. (electro plate Britannia metal).

From the collector's point of view there is still time to gather interesting pieces at reasonable price. Anything made in silver could be made in Britannia metal and silver designs were copied, so there are some quite nice shapes. It is hard to find a piece which has the original shine. Usually, it looks like pewter and has often been bought and sold as such. Many of the teapots made in Britannia metal have become damaged by the practice in the past of keeping the pot warm, for the metal has a low melting point when in contact with flame. I have seen a number of pieces with melt damage and it is impossible to repair them.

Was pewter silver plated at any time, and, if so, when? We have an old pewter teapot which shows some traces of plate. The only mark is EPBM on the base. The body is engraved.

Your teapot is certainly Britannia metal. This material was used from about 1790. The process was much cheaper to produce than Sheffield plate. The quality varied, the best being 90% tin, 8% antimony, and 2% copper, which could be highly polished in the manner of silver. It was easy to produce useful ware by casting in moulds or by diestamping. From about 1820, hollow ware was made by lathe spinning. Collectors can still find a good selection of Britannia metal, meat dish covers, toast racks, tea and coffee ware, tankards, hot water jugs, fruit baskets, candlesticks, to name but a few. The metal resembles pewter and is a hard form of that metal. If struck with a wood dowel it gives a ringing tone.

One characteristic of Britannia metal is that once the original polished brightness is allowed to get dull and oxydise, it cannot be entirely brought back. EPBM on the pot described means Electro Plate on Britannia metal, the process becoming popular after about 1850. Items were made quite cheaply and the plating did not last very well, reverting to the pewter look fairly quickly. The best pieces to look for are those made by firms like John Vickers and James Dixon of Sheffield; these pieces are marked.

6   Glass

Looking around for something to collect which would not be too difficult to find, and be fairly easy on the pocket, decanters seemed to fit the bill. They look nice on the sideboard and displayed in a cabinet. So far nothing really spectacular has come to hand, but I have a rather nice pair with flattish stoppers which are star cut at the top. The base is also star cut but the most attractive feature is the cutting on the bowl. There are several ovals with slices cut to the base of the decanter, and when viewed from any direction these cuttings appear as wine glasses. The bases have scratch wear consistent with long use. Would these decanters be of 18th century date?

One of a pair of Georgian decanters

This is quite a pleasant pair of baluster decanters. It is quite an unusual cutting which you describe. The photograph shows the wine glass shapes running round the bowl.

In the 17th century, wine was contained in dark green and brown bottles which were quite nicely shaped, and wine was taken to the table in the bottle. These bottles, particularly those with a personal seal, are now collected. The first clear glass decanters came along as the results of experiments by George Ravenscroft, and early flint glass decanters were made, taking the form of jugs with a beaked spout. Flint glass examples from about 1670 are very rare. The jug developed into a bottle shape in cruciform and stoppers were blown glass. Old decanters have a lipped neck intended to secure the string holding the stoppers. The name decanter seems to have crept in during the early 18th century and stoppered examples, as we know them, from about 1735. Allowing for reproductions, decanters can be dated from their shape and the style of stopper, and it will help you if you read the works specialising in the subject. Stoppers should be a perfect fit and most are ground in; if a stopper fails to fit properly it generally means that it has been changed. Stoppers do sometimes become jammed in and the worst thing you can do is to try and tap them free; this invariably means a break. Removing a stopper is a three-handed job. With someone holding the decanter, wrap a piece of string once round the top of the neck and with a sawing motion create frictional heat, which will expand the neck and allow the stopper to be withdrawn.

Having given a useful hint, I have to say that your decanters are not 18th but 19th century. If you are collecting specimens of this quality you are on the right lines. There are coloured decanters worth including in a collection, and to find a single or pair of Bristol blue with labels in gilt, would give you pleasure. They were made about 1800 with pinched stoppers, and any decanter collection will be enhanced by their inclusion.

We have a three bottle tantalus with an oak frame and plated mounts. It has a locking device, but unfortunately the key is missing. It was bought for a few pounds a number of years ago. Is it of any particular value today. Do you know how they came to be called 'tantalus'?

A three-bottle tantalus

The three bottle tantalus was popular in the 19th century. Quite a number were used as presentation pieces as they are often found with inscription plates. They are of value and at the time of writing some are making around three figures. It is always as well to examine carefully before buying, to make certain that the decanters match and are not later replacements. (I have seen some tantalus with pressed glass replacement bottles.) The ground-in stoppers should all match and beware of small chips on the lips.

It is difficult to know exactly how a name occurs. Perhaps in this case it may well have been taken from a mythological character, 'Tantalus', father of Pelops, who, when admitted to a banquet of the gods incurred their displeasure by betraying their secrets. As a punishment he was condemned to suffer the pangs of thirst and hunger, by being placed in water up to his neck in such a way that he could not drink or take nearby food, without dislodging a huge rock suspended above him which would have crushed him to death. The tantalus lock prevents the stoppers being removed from the bottles, so you can see the drink but not partake of it until the host produces the key. This was more a deterrent than a punishment, for no doubt it was intended to prevent the household staff from taking the odd nip of the master's spirits. Bottles take the square form to fit the frame, which are usually in wood with metal mounts, although some are found in all-plate frames. The square hobnail cut bottles with globular brilliant stoppers seem to be interchangeable with any frame and were produced for that purpose. Some decanters have numbers on the stopper and decanter neck, in order to ensure perfect fit. The White-friars Glass Works customarily did this on the decanters produced by them.

Every Victorian middle class home probably sported a tantalus and I suppose every collector's home will continue the tradition.

Is it possible to discover the age of a decanter? It is quite heavy with a barrel shaped body, cut lines in panels on four sides. There are raised cut bands on the shoulder and base. The neck has several step cuts, the stopper is flat. There are wear scratches on the base rim.

Decanters have changed shapes in different defined periods, but there is no certainty of dating from the shape, due to constant reproduction. The barrel shape seemed to emerge during the last quarter of the 18th century. Stoppers, also changed and some guide can be given about these. Blown stoppers date from the early 18th century; disc, cone, lozenge and pear shape date from the last quarter of the 18th century. Mushroom, target and cut globe shapes date from the first quarter of the 19th century.

The description you give with the flat or mushroom stopper suggests early 19th century and the obvious base wear supports this. Decanters were the natural follow-on from Italian wine flasks and came into popular use during the 18th century, being more attractive on the table than the dark brown and green wine bottles. Early decanters were stopped with corks and have a string ring near the top of the neck but very few of these survive.

Some decanters are found to be very stained, if wine dregs have been left over a period. If normal methods fail to remove the stains, try an old fashioned remedy which seems to work. Peel a potato finely, cut-up and pack the pieces into the decanter. Allow the potato to stand for three of four days to ferment. Remove the peel and wash the decanter out with clean water.

Old drinking glasses have taken my fancy and I would like to make a collection of them, particularly as I have a nice pair of corner cupboards in which to display them. I have bought only one or two so far and wonder if I am proceeding along the right lines. One has a cotton twist stem with a plain bowl, another with plain stem and engraved bowl. Both bowls are similar in shape; both have rough bases. Is this usual?

18th century cordial glasses

Putting together a collection of English drinking glasses should give you great pleasure and there åre reference works to help you. Air twist stems are an English innovation and seem to have appeared on the scene just before 1740. They developed from the earlier tear stem glasses which were contrived by denting and then laying on more glass to trap a quantity of air. The air twist effect may have been discovered more by accident than design. The opaque twist was certainly by design and made easier by making glasses in three parts, (bowl, stem and foot made separately). It was not long before two opaque rods could be laid in the mould and, when drawn and twisted, the fine lacework patterns were controlled to great effect. Opaque twist remained popular until the 1780's and thankfully, a great number of examples have survived.

The bottoms can be quite rough due to the breaking off of the pontil or punty rod used by the glass maker to dip and hold the molten glass while shaping the base. The bowl shape on both the cordial glasses is known as double ogee; the feet are nicely domed. Of 18th century date, they have got you off to a good start.

Wine glasses offer you a very wide range of styles, but it must be said that some of the early and more rare pieces can be quite expensive. However, with a little study and experience you will have the opportunity to gather some nice pieces in the reasonable range, and often you will find odd bargains. Display is all-important and you have the right idea. There are old glasses in green, blue and cranberry which can add lustre to a collection.

A few Christmasses ago I was given a paper weight by an old lady, who told me that it had been in her family for many years, and she remembered being told not to touch it when she was a little girl. It is very attractive with lacework and what I think are called 'canes', with animals and birds on the top. One of the canes has a small number 1847 on it. The base shows wear as seen on old pieces of glass which have been moved round a lot. I would like to know how old it really is.

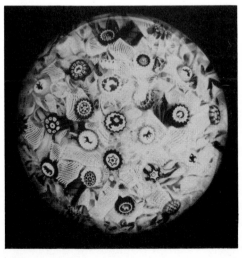

A Baccarat paper weight c. 1847

Paper weights became very popular in the 19th century. Sparked off by the Venetian glass makers, other countries followed suit. The French glass houses went into production in a quite substantial way and produced many of the pieces found in collections today. Baccarat, Clichy and St. Louis were prominent and produced beautiful weights in various designs, the most popular being 'Millifiore' with multiple flower heads, as the name suggests, using all the colours of the spectrum. Other designs included reptiles, single flowers and insects. The majority were of mushroom shape but there were other shapes and overlay was featured. (Ink bottles and vases with millifiore bases can also be found.)

Paper weights were also made in Britain around the same period, at places like Stourbridge. There still remains a thriving business in quality paper weights and glass houses like Whitefriars and Caithness produce general and limited editions in the traditional way. There are a large number of inferior weights about but quality, or lack of it, speaks for itself. Many of these are imported from the far east and have rather flooded the market. In the main these are not very expensive, but it is feasible that some may be marked at fancy prices which, in this case, ensures that you will not get what you pay for. Old paper weights command fairly high prices, and even modern pieces from quality makers in special and limited editions usually have certificates with them and can cost upwards of fifty pounds.

The gift you received is one of the prime collector's weights, being an early 'Baccarat' with meandering Latticino ground. These were dated 1846 to 1849, the 1848 date being more usual among the survivors. Your paper weight, dated 1847, is less common. 1849 seems to be the more rare of the dated pieces.

Paper weights offer a wide range to the collector and nothing looks nicer in multiple display than these beautiful and colourful objects.

We have rather ususual glass object. It is 6 inches long and resembles an Indian club in shape, or perhaps a small decanter. There is a rim at the top of the neck with a small hole which we assume is for pouring, but there is a hole in the base too, so it would not hold liquid. It has slice cutting as seen on some decanters. Can you explain its use?

From the 17th century, great bowls of punch or toddy were popular and were normally served with a ladle. Punch was introduced from the Far East by the Dutch. The Indian name is 'panch', being Hindi for five, which makes up the essential ingredients and included arrack spirit, tea, spices, fruit juices and hot water. According to the ingredients, European punch is called rum, whisky or brandy punch. Milk, wine or ale can also be added.

No one knows exactly when the 'toddy lifter' was invented but it is credited to a Scot. Now you know what your strange piece is. You might well ask 'How does it serve punch?' If the lifter is placed into a bowl of liquid it starts to fill. When a finger or thumb is placed over the hole at the top, the pipette system comes into effect and the liquid is held. Hold the lifter over the glass, remove the finger from the hole at the top and, hey presto, the liquid pours into the glass.

Toddy lifters were made through the 18th into the 19th century. Very early ones are museum pieces, but the later cut pieces can take their rightful place in a glass collection, or might even be collected as a separate section.

It would be interesting to know when glass lustre vases came on the scene. We have a pair in red glass which have been in the family for the past seventy or eighty years. They are 12 inches high and in perfect condition.

A glass lustre vase

At the great Exhibition held in London in 1851, the Neuwelt Bohemian glass works, (then under the direction of Count Harrach), exhibited coloured lustre vases. These caught the imagination of the Victorians and they immediately became popular. The Europeans had the monopoly, but it was not long before English firms realised the potential and went into production on a large scale, to meet the growing demand, which continued into the Edwardian period. It would have been difficult to enter an ordinary home without seeing at least one pair of lustre vases on the mantelpiece or sideboard. Lustre vases are sometimes referred to as musical or windtone, for when moved the prisms produce tinkling tones of different pitch. The vases were made in several colours, green, blue, red, pink and opaque white with painted decoration. The best looking pieces are those in overlay. This was achieved by laying coloured glass over clear, then grinding and polishing through the outer glass to form patterns, some with added gilt decoration. All the vases mainly follow the same style, with serrated or waved edge bowls, vase or column stems on a foot. Many vases were stripped of prisms after the second world war and were used to make up light fitments, often passed off as Regency. These found a ready market during a period of great austerity. Although prisms do have a light reflection quality, they seem to have filled a more ornamental role and were used purely for that purpose. They were the fashion and that was enough for the Victorians.

Collectors like to have a pair of lustre vases, for they are attractive and with the growing scarcity will be hard to come by in a few years. This is one of the areas in which you can acquire the best looking, by spotting and swopping, (what we call in the trade, 'growing' a good pair for your personal collection.)

Having decided that our main collective interest will be glass, and rather than collect odd pieces of all sorts, we would like to concentrate on glass from a single source. Can you advise on how best to develop our efforts in this field?

The great name which comes to mind is Ravenscroft English full lead crystal which was invented in 1676, the patent being released to other glass houses in 1685. However, Ravenscroft glass, apart from being very rare, might well be beyond the reach of the ordinary collector. Another great name which comes to mind is Whitefriars, established in the 17th century during the reign of Charles II on the banks of the Thames near the Temple, on a site which had previously been occupied by a monastery. The Carmelite Fathers were known as Whitefriars and the glass house borrowed the name, which is retained to the present day.

In the year 1710 advertisements appeared which invited customers to the glass house to buy all sorts of glass which could be made to special pattern at reasonable rates. (One can still see a similar advertisement for the Whitefriars furnaces, which have never been allowed to go out, even when the factory was transferred to its present works at Wealdstone in the county of Middlesex, in 1923. A brazier was brought from London to ignite the new furnaces, so the flames have burnt continuously for nearly 300 years). Walking round the glass house today, one can see workmen using the same tools and the same skill as in the 17th century. Special designs are made to customers' order, like Freeman's caskets made for the Borough of Harrow.

Examples of work from Whitefriars. Above, decanters. Below left, 1977
Jubilee paper weights. Right, a Millefiore inkwell

Since 1840 millefiore paperweights have provided a challenge to glassmakers and the Whitefriars' craftsmen have produced some fine examples. Their commemoratives too offer a range to collectors and include the Mayflower centenary, Olympic games, Bicentenary of American Independence, and Queen Elizabeth II's Jubilee. Whitefriars paperweights are dated and carry the mark of a Friar. Some fifty different examples can be collected, together with inkwells and decanters with millefiore stoppers. There is a large range of 19th and 20th century decanters with marked, matching stoppers, (tiny numbers on the neck and stopper base).

Whitefriars is also famous for its stained glass. The Adam and Eve frieze in St. Paul's Cathedral, London, was created by Whitefriars in 1800 and the great chandeliers in the Assembly Rooms at Bath were made at Whitefriars in 1779. This glass house used fine white sand from Fontainebleau with red lead and potash to produce fine brilliant crystal.

Beautiful windows can also be seen in St. Thomas's Church, Fifth Avenue, New York, and at St. Barnabas Church, Mount Lebanon, Pennsylvania. The stained glass in Wellington Cathedral, New Zealand, is also a showpiece.

The first furnaces were fired with wood, then seacoal, in the 18th century, switching to oil in the 1930's. Fireclay pots were made in the factory to withstand temperatures of around one thousand degrees; the life of a pot is fifteen weeks, the life of a furnace just over twenty years, during which time it burns continuously. Glass making tools have not changed over the centuries, the craftsmen, as in years gone by, gather the molten glass on the blowing iron by rotating it in the furnace, by rolling or 'maivering', it is centred on the iron to obtain a smooth shape and the creation of another fine piece of glassware is commenced.

The factory houses its own museum with a fine collection presided over by the present Chief Designer, Geoffrey Baxter, and arrangements can be made to view and to tour the glass house, which looks very much the same as when it first started. Whitefriars have adhered to the ancient methods and their wares, often in limited editions, become collectors' pieces. With the Whitefriar mark, you will be able to identify work from this factory.

7   Boxes

We have a Tunbridge ware jewel box in our possession. It is made up of cubes and mosaic inlay work in different colours. The inside has compartments and it measures 10 inches by 5 inches. How did this work get the name?

Tunbridge ware

Tunbridge ware is a general name given to block and mosaic work in wood, but it is not all from that area in Kent.

Tunbridge Wells was a spa from the 17th century, much visited by people who could afford to take the waters. The town became a busy centre for the work, particularly from the early 19th century.

As with all areas which attract visitors, local craftsmen seized the opportunity to make a good living providing souvenirs, and as there had been a woodworking industry in the area for many years, it followed that the skill would be used in creating items for sale to visitors. The smaller items were called toys, but they did not stop there. The designs ranged from lucifer boxes to standard chairs, tables, trays and pictures. There is a tremendous range for the collector. Woods used in design included holly, cherry, yew, sycamore, fruitwood and imported Lignum Vitae, and the effect is delightful.

Before about 1820 the work was in block form. After this period mosaic came into use. It may have followed the Sorento wood mosaic which appeared in the early 19th century. Italian work is often mistaken for Tunbridge, but if the Italian mosaic is carefully examined, the lines wave about a bit and are not as precise.

(The Italians also used a lot of wood dye and the results look artificial.)

The cutting of small pieces of veneer took time and was therefore costly to produce. The market was starting to demand a cheaper commodity. As people other than the wealthy began to visit Tunbridge Wells it became necessary to devise a cheaper way of producing the ware. About 1850, different woods were pressed and glued together forming a pattern which ran right through, (rather like the wording in seaside rock). Veneer could be sliced from the end of the block and then glued to the body material. Even so, it was still quite time consuming to cut slices no more than one sixteenth of an inch in thickness. This technique produced what is known as 'end grain mosaic'.

It is the workmanship of Tunbridge ware which has attracted collectors, and no doubt the collection made by the well known collector of treen, Edward Pinto, which he allowed the public to see at his house in Northwood, Middlesex, did much to arouse interest. The late Edward Pinto's collection is now housed at the Birmingham Museum and of course there is a fine collection at the museum in Tunbridge Wells.

Not having made a point of collecting tea caddies, I would like to know the approximate date of the one I do possess. It is in rosewood with two lift-out box compartments, both with hinged lids. The centre well is shaped and turned but does not lift out. The handles are rather pretty, carved like seashells, and the body is slightly shaped on turned feet.

A Georgian rosewood tea chest

There are collectors who specialise in tea chests and caddies but in the main one finds that people who have pieces of antique furniture in the home also have one or two examples of these items. This rosewood tea chest of the Georgian period dates at circa 1800. Rosewood started being popular in the late 18th century and remained so for a few years. Tea chests were an essential part of the furnishing of a home in this period and were often cabinet made to match the furniture. Designers such as Hepplewhite and Sheraton concerned themselves with them. 'Chest' was the term used for the pieces with compartments: these were made for those who preferred to blend the leaf. The centre well may have had a fitted glass container specially shaped, (some did not), but it is rare to find a chest with the original glass, which could often be a piece of Waterford. Most have disappeared or have been replaced with an inferior quality. No doubt some blending glasses were removed and used for other purposes, as some of the chests became workboxes or receptacles for bits and pieces.

The occasional chest can be found with a vesta compartment and a brass striking plate, (for use with the spirit kettle). We do not often hear a match called 'vesta' these days, a word from Roman mythology associated with the Greek Goddess of the hearth who was worshipped in recognition of the supreme importance of fire. The Temple, Atrium Vestae was built in her honour, it is said the sacred fire which burned there was brought from Troy.

Single boxes, namely caddies, were made for those not keen to blend. Caddies and chests were made in large quantities mainly in wood, but also in silver and Sheffield plate. Only the metal type are still used occasionally for holding tea.

Incidentally, the tin tea caddies of a few years ago find their devotees among collectors these days.

An elderly aunt has given my small son a money box. It must be fairly old as I remember playing with it as a child. It is made of iron in the form of a negro page boy, half figure; he wears a red coat and bow tie. The hand is shaped to hold a coin and when a lever at the back is pressed, his eyes move and the coin is popped into the mouth. How old would this money box be?

Money boxes offer a wide field to the collector. No one really knows when they first came on the scene. There is evidence that they were around in the 16th and 17th centuries. Money boxes in some form might well have been used ever since there were coins to put in them.

Many of the varieties which were made in china and clay have not survived for the simple reason that it was necessary to break them to retrieve the coins. These were made in different forms, hens, dogs, etc., and we all remember the good old piggy bank. Some 18th

A 19th century blackamoor mechanical money box

century pieces in the form of cottages have survived, and might still be discovered, and there were many interesting pieces produced by country studio potteries. Mechanical boxes, known throughout the 19th century, reached a peak during the period from the 1880's to 1890's.

The principal areas of manufacture were Germany, Switzerland and the United States of America. Some boxes were made in the British midlands — the hoopla Toby dog is one of the rare English pieces. The United States of America was early in the field of mechanical money boxes. The Artillery Bank first produced one about 1812. It comprised a cannon which was loaded with a coin and, when triggered, the coin was shot into the fort. Shooting pieces were favoured by boys and both rifles and crossbow examples exist, the coin usually fired into the stump of a tree. Some of the boxes have ingenious mechanism, other have simple levers. There are also a number of boxes representing banks. The American firm, J. & A. Stevens, made bank boxes from the middle of the 19th century. The Japanese also produced mechanical boxes powered by a battery.

Most mechanical boxes are in cast iron and quite heavy. In this century copies were made in aluminium.

Your negro or blackamoor box dates circa 1860. Perhaps you might guide your son into the money box collecting field. All boxes have some interest, and those made today will be the collectors' items of the future.

We have a rather unusual item the use of which has been much discussed, but so far no definite conclusion has been reached. It is made of a reddish brown wood and takes the form of a pair of high boots mounted on a flat base, with small feet. There is a pattern of inlay of mother of pearl and brass. The top has a sliding panel with a compartment beneath. Can you solve the problem?

This is an inlaid mahogany 'snuff box' not for the pocket but for the table. In the 18th and early 19th century, snuff taking was the prerogative of gentlemen; each tried to outdo the other by possessing a beautiful box. Later in the 19th century the habit became more widespread and consequently more utility boxes came into use.

Hand carved and beautifully made, the box described dates circa 1860 and is suitable to include in a collection.

My grandfather collected unusual boxes, some of which have now been handed down to me. I did not have much interest in them before so I know very little about them, but since having the boxes in my house, I find them quite fascinating. The ones I find most mystifying are those which are made in the shape of fruit: the apples are 5 inches to 6 inches high, the pears 7 inches high. They are beautifully turned and polished. They all have hinged lids and are fitted with tiny locks but I do not have the keys. Some have carved stem knobs, others are made of ivory. There is evidence of silver paper inside some. Does this point to any special use?

A pearwood tea caddy   *An applewood tea caddy*

You have a good and rare collection of apple and pearwood tea caddies, dating 18th or early 19th century, I would think. These are quite different from the usual tea caddies we generally see and are country craft, made with some skill. Other fruitwoods were also used — together with birch, burr, beech, boxwood — and also the very hard Lignum Vitae. These caddies can be found in several fruit forms including melon.

Any collector of tea caddies would find the inclusion of these a delight.

It is amazing the great variety of vessels which were used for keeping the tea leaf in good condition. Most have locks and the keys were held by the lady of the house to prevent wasteful use of tea by household staff. You are fortunate in your inheritance, and truly can enjoy the fruits of your grandfather's labour!

Among a small collection of odds and ends, we have a small box made of ivory. The lid is studded with gold and the centre panel is raised and decorated with gold and enamel. The inside is velvet-lined, with a mirror in the lid. Its purpose has been the subject of discussion and the general opinion is that it is a lady's patch box. Can you shed any light on it?

From the description I do not think this is a lady's patch box, which I admit has similar characteristics. I can imagine this box in the pocket of a Regency gentleman and containing silver or gold tooth picks. You have quite a rare little box and you may be fortunate enough to discover a Georgian toothpick one day to keep in it.

In the main, most toothpicks available are those which were made for the watch chain, in engine-turned cases with a retractable diamond shaped pick. Small unusual boxes can make an interesting subject for collection. They can be found without too much problem coming up in small lots at auction, and most antique and curio shops have examples on display. For not too great an outlay a good collection can be made. Some thought must be given to display and an Edwardian specimen table is ideal for the purpose, for you need to look down to obtain the full effect. I have seen long coffee tables made to order by a cabinet maker in Chippendale or Queen Anne styles, with lift-up plate glass tops and velvet lined wells. These are fine for small displays and have a dual purpose.

I have among my collection of miscellaneous items two rather unusual boxes and have not seen anything quite like them anywhere. One is made in mahogany in an octagonal shape, with a conical panel lid which has a carved rose forming the handle. The lid fits quite firmly and is hinged. The other is a six-sided box and all the panels are filled with tightly rolled paper arranged to form flowers and running patterns. The lid is also hinged and has a small brass handle. Both the boxes show signs of being fairly old and it would be interesting to know when they were made, and for what purpose they would have been used.

Left, *a mahogany tea caddy.*
Above, *a paper tea caddy*

The mahogany box is certainly not a commercial piece. Most probably it was a 'one off' or it may have a partner somewhere. It is the sort of thing which starts with the thought 'I must make something' and with a few tools and odd pieces of wood, a useful and quite attractive item is the result. I have a passion for making bird boxes out of odd bits of wood and we all have a go at making something at one time or another. This chap, whoever he was, thought of a tea caddy and the result is the subject of your question. It is difficult to say when it was made, but being in the Sheraton style suggests a late 18th, early 19th century date.

The other box is also the result of a singular hobby, using paper as the main decorative material. I have not seen another like it either. The time and patience involved to roll and set each scroll in position to form the picture suggests that it was decorated by a young lady. In the early 19th century there was quite an interest in hand work, particularly in the creation of embroidery pictures, with features and other parts often painted. The tiny handle is probably original and is of the type seen on Sheraton-style pieces, early 19th century, and it suggests that sort of date for this tea caddy. If you are considering making a collection of unusual boxes, (and this can be of great interest), you have made a very good start with these two pieces.

It would be interesting to know the date of an oval tea caddy which I have had for a long time. The wood is quite light and silky in colour. The lid is inlaid with flowers and there is a round inlay on the front. The keyhole surround is of ivory and the interior is foil lined. It is in perfect condition.

A Sheraton satinwood tea caddy

Tea caddies are attractive and particularly an example like this, which is made in satinwood, one of the rarer woods used at the end of the 18th century and favoured by makers like Sheraton. The marquetry is interesting for it shows the convolvulus, a popular flower in the period, but which is seldom seen in flower gardens today, (except the variety which is a troublesome weed). There was a reason for cultivation in years gone by. This plant had a medicinal property and was used in what we now term 'folk medicine'.

You have quite a rare tea caddy in the Sheraton style dating circa 1790.

My grandfather was a doctor and he, like others in the profession in his day, received presents from grateful patients. He also told me that it was not unusual to be offered items of value in place of cash to cover the bill, in the country district where he practised for many years. When he died there was quite a collection to be shared among the family. One of the pieces which came to me is a gold box. It is beautifully chased and embossed. The lid shows a landscape with two retriever dogs in the foreground and a man with a gun in the distance. The mark has mostly disappeared and all that remains is the figure '18' and a king's head facing right. It weighs about two and a half ounces troy. Can you possibly date it from what remains of the hallmark?

Your grandfather's story about doctors receiving payment in kind has been substantiated by older doctors with whom I have come in contact. I once met one who had retired after many years of practice in the Lake District. He told me that more often than not he knew it was useless to present a bill and was often paid in kind. If he admired an ornament or similar during a visit, it usually ended up as part or whole payment of his bill. He pointed out quite a number of things in

A Georgian gold snuff box

his house which had come to him through the system. Barter has not completely died out in country districts today.

This is a fine 18ct gold snuff box and it is a pity that so little of the mark remains. Unfortunately, most monarch head marks face to the right. George III faced left for only a very short period in the 18th century, and Queen Victoria faced left throughout her reign. Snuff boxes were much used by the Georgians and the constant use of a soft metal causes it to wear. Habitual snuff takers handle their boxes quite a bit. From the style, and what remains of the mark, this box is of George III's period, circa 1815. It is a charming antique piece, and the weight makes it a very valuable heirloom.

Some years ago my father bought a mahogany tea caddy of which he has rather a high opinion and says it is 18th century. It looks so perfect that I wonder if he is right about it, and I think it would have shown some damage after being around a kitchen all that time. He keeps it on the sideboard now. It is very nice with a carved edge all round, which looks like rope, and still has a key which works. Would it be really as old as my father thinks?

A Georgian mahogany tea caddy with carved rope edge

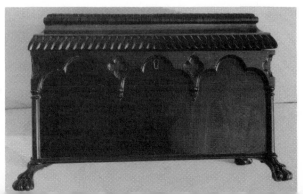

Your father is right to think a lot of this piece. It is beautifully made and is 18th century. It was probably made by the same cabinet maker who produced the rest of the house furnishings in its day. Accessories, like barometers and tea caddies, were often treated as part of the furniture design. Unlike today, when tea caddies are kept in a kitchen cupboard, these old caddies were kept in the dining room, so this one is still in its rightful place. The rope edging is an added feature and a similar effect was used on old Sheffield plate to hide the edges. The bell top, as it is called, is very similar to the tops of some old bracket clocks; these too were cabinet made. This is a delightful tea caddy, which I hope you will also cherish.

See below a fine example with carved paw feet, and turned pillasters which emphasises the amount of work in these pieces.

A Georgian mahogany tea caddy on carved paw feet

8   Gramophones and Radios

I have recently taken an interest in old gramophones and now have three in my collection. One is a cylinder machine. Can you offer any information about a Columbia gramophone which has the original horn and cover and plays cylinders. Are cylinders for these machines still available and where would be the best place to obtain them?

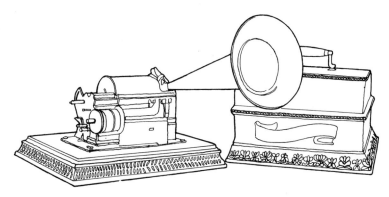

A cylinder gramophone

Thomas Edison started it all when he shouted into a machine and like many important inventions it all came about by accident. He was at the time working on a machine and concerned with the recording of the morse code by a series of dots on paper. I do not know what made him do it, but he shouted into the machine and must have been quite amazed with he heard his voice come back. As a result, he got to work on a reproduction machine and by 1877 he was recording on a piece of tin foil wrapped round a cardboard cylinder and the phonograph was born. A patent was taken out for a gramophone in 1886, and sounds were recorded and reproduced on wax cylinders.

The Columbia Company were early in the field and in 1894 were the first to perfect a motor with a governed spring which would allow an even tension right through the playing time. The Columbia machines have a strong resemblance to treadle sewing machine tops for the very good reason that Columbia had bought out a sewing machine company, and the treadle tops and covers were readily available and suited the purpose of housing a gramophone. By the end of the 19th century many firms were going strong — Edison, Columbia, Pathe and the Gramophone Company later to become H.M.V. — among them. Although the flat disc came on the scene as a result of experiments by Emil Berliner, a German who emigrated to the United

States, the cylinders remained popular and as there was a vast amount of machines to use them, the manufacture continued well into the 1920's. There must be still quite a large quantity around. I have seen collections of them appear in auctions in recent years. You have to take pot luck if you buy a batch as there is no way of testing the quality.

There now exist quite a number of dealer collectors of cylinders and these are probably the best source for the better material if you want perfection. One of the main problems is storage space, for cylinders have to be kept in reasonable conditions. Damp is one of the biggest enemies and a mildewed cylinder is useless. The Columbia machines are quite prized and the rare models like the AB type hard to find.

Can you advise if two old radio sets are worth keeping, and might they eventually become collectors' pieces? One is in a polished rosewood case in church window shape. The speaker is fronted with a fretwork design, three wavy lines and four starlike crosses. The other is in a mahogany case of squarish design with a low pitched top. The speaker front is a fretwork sunray with clouds. About what date are they?

The early radio sets have already become collectors' items among a few admirers. Museums have been interested for some time and are building collections. The earlier set with horn similar to the gramophone of the 1922 period is certainly rising very quickly in value and there is quite good competition for them at auction. Developed from the original 'cat's whisker' crystal sets, the wireless became a valued instrument and required a case for protection. It was not long before speakers became incorporated and a more furniture-like cabinet came on the market. Furniture designers were brought in, one of the first being Gordon Russell, a British designer from the Cotswolds.

Most early cabinets had front designs which could be readily associated with the makers of the sets. The cabinet first mentioned is a Phillips' model of 1932 vintage. The other is a Pye and dates 1932. In the 1930's several firms were in competition for a very lucrative market, and the cabinet design became an important selling factor. Most cabinets were made of wood, bakelite beginning to be used about 1936. The war years produced the 'utility' set, all with the same simple cabinet, but excellent in their receiving quality, and the 1944 set will no doubt take its place in a collection.

After the second world war, there was a market for more flamboyant design and the 'Ebor' globe set was produced in 1946. It was of futuristic design and a floor standing model, similar to the standard lamp pedestal. I think this model is quite rare today.

There must be quite a number of pre-war wireless sets sitting up in lofts all over the country. Now is the time to retrieve them and, if damp has not damaged them, they may again become a status symbol as an interior decoration and become collectors' pieces.

Are old disc gramophones worth keeping and when were the flat records first made? We have a table model made by the 'Gramophone and Typewriter Company' in an oak case. It has quite a large brass horn. We do not have any records for it, but the spring is sound.

A disc gramophone

If you do decide to dispose of it, there are a number of keen collectors these days. The greatest problem for collectors is space for display, for you can eventually acquire rows of them. I think a single model is worth retaining, particularly one with a brass horn, which was an optional extra. The company which produced this machine adopted the famous 'Dog and Horn' trade mark and became the great H.M.V. Company. This model was supplied with a carved oak pedestal cabinet for storing records, and the instrument was kept on the top.

The invention of the first flat disc is credited to Emil Berliner in 1891. It was pressed in Hanover and early discs were single-sided. To have a gramophone like this without records is not very fulfilling. Seventy-eight records can still be picked up. One has to be selective, for many are badly worn and scratched. Good early recordings are rare and can be expensive.

Quantities of records can be found at jumble sales, and sometimes come up at auction but you take your chance. I once bought a lot of three hundred, but only two were really worth having. It all depends on how much a perfectionist you are.

If you do play good early records on this machine, it is far better to use a thorn needle rather than steel. Steel needles can be damaging while the thorn are much kinder to the grooves.

Both cylinder and disc machines are much sought after and in the last few years values have risen quite considerably. This is another example of non-antiques forging ahead of their time. There are more collectors than ever now and thank goodness for that, for it ensures the preservation of much that would have been destroyed. That is what conservation is all about.

9 Clocks and Watches and Scientific Instruments

Having acquired a French carriage clock we are anxious to know more about them. The one we have has a brass case decorated with Cloisonne enamel. Although only 6½ inches tall it is quite heavy. There are no marks on the movement. The people who sold it to us said they thought it was antique. Were these clocks made in the 18th century?

A 19th century French carriage clock

Travelling clocks were actually made quite early. Thomas Tompion, one of Britain's finest clockmakers (1639-1713), made clocks designed for travelling. In those days the balance wheel hair spring system was not sophisticated enough to ensure reliable timekeeping, so two systems were fitted, which allowed the pendulum to be levered out of action for travelling. When the clock was at rest, the more reliable pendulum action was brought into play. Travel clocks in the 18th century had more the appearance of a giant watch, and these had a leather case to protect them during the very rough rides experienced in unsprung coaches and bad roads.

The travel clock as we know it today did not evolve until the 19th century and very few date before 1850. It was a few years before brass and glazed carriage clocks were mass produced. Some of the 19th century examples still have their specially made leather-covered cases, but many have been discarded along the way as a result of these timepieces being used as house clocks.

It is doubtful if many of these clocks have actually been on a journey. Carriage clocks were very popular in the second half of the 19th century and the majority of them were not very expensive. They were not particularly well thought of a few years ago and prices were quite low. Now things have changed and carriage clocks have come into favour among collectors and, in consequence, prices have risen quite substantially. The popularity is manifested by the large number being made by modern clockmakers, (still, I might add, by mass production). There are exceptions of course, and you get what you pay for. The quality of both 19th and 20th century carriage clocks varies. Those with repeat movements are more favoured and silver cases can be found.

This example, with Cloisonné work and rather nicely turned pilasters at each corner, with break front and vase feet, is one of the more interesting examples of a Paris-made clock, circa 1880. It is as well when buying a carriage clock to look for something a little bit different from the run of the mill; the extra cost is worthwhile. English examples would be my first choice. I have seen carriage clocks with porcelain panel sides coming up in auction. These should not be taken for granted, however, as those I saw were not original. It is always as well to record clock numbers in case of loss. It does help with identification. Carriage clocks often have a number on the edge of the door frame but is not easy to see.

It would be interesting to know a little about a striking clock in a mahogany case which is delicately inlaid with brass scrollwork. The top is in drape style shaped like the roof of a pagoda. The sides have brass openwork panels and ring handles. The base has a moulded edge with brass bracket feet.

A Regency bracket clock

This is a very attractive bracket clock of the Regency period. Earlier bracket clocks were intended to be portable and carried from room to room as required. The handles were quite substantial to support the weight of the clock. Later the clocks were left on side tables or mantel pieces and the handles, some on the sides rather than the top, took on a lighter and more decorative look. Shapes of bracket clocks have changed very little. Tops vary being basket shaped, arched, architectural, or fancy. Decorative finials are often seen added purely for decoration. The movements are always of very good quality because clockmakers were precision engineers, working incidentally, without the aid of machinery.

The clock in question made by James Milne of Montrose, Scotland, and dating circa 1810. Maintenance of clocks is often neglected, and they are left to run for years and years without being serviced. Like all other machinery they do require a regular check by a clockmaker, if excess wear to bushes and other parts is to be avoided. It is as well to remember that there is only one oil for a clock, and that is clock oil, applied by the hands of an expert.

Watches have always fascinated me and for years I could never resist buying a gold or silver example. It is only recently that I have started to take stock and go through them. One in particular seems to be very interesting. It is quite small with a gold case. The face is white enamel with a ring of engraving and white enamel beads round the edge of the bezel. The hour hand is in a delicate fleur de lis shape. The back is enamelled in blue, white, brown and green with two cherubs, one holding the sword and the other the scales of justice. It is rather tricky to open. Inside is the maker's name, Jeffreys and Jones, London, a crowned leopard and a lion and initials T.P. Is it possible to say what year it was made? It has a very fine chain drive and the balance wheel has a beautifully chased cover. I am also interested to know about another watch in gold case, maker's name Vulliamy, London. It has an inner case which is scroll engraved and marked with 18 crown over the top, small letter 'a', crowned leopard's head and initials F.H. It has a repeating strike movement and the face is white enamel with a convex glass. Can you confirm that it is George III period?

Your passion for watches over the years has no doubt resulted in a fascinating collection, some of which could be quite valuable. The fob watch is a very nice Georgian example. The makers, Jeffreys and Jones, working from Cockspur Street, London, are known for richly decorated watches and this gold and enamel case is a good example. They were usually worn on a swivel and ribbon, with a seal protruding from the pocket. The watch has an English fuseé movement and in these very small pieces, the making of such a fine chain is a feat of

Above, *back view of a Georgian fob or pocket watch*. Left, *the front of the same watch*. Right, *a Georgian pocket watch with repeater*

engineering and clockmaker's skill. Early watches open in a different way to their modern counterparts, the movement being housed in its independent ring released by a tiny press spring on the edge of the case. Trying to prise open a case causes considerable damage. The gold chain shown with the watch is later, of 19th century date. Georgian fob watch ribbons can still be found with amethyst or cornelian seal ends.

The gold pocket watch with repeater movement by Vulliamy is quite interesting. Justine Vulliamy left Switzerland to work in Britain in 1730. His son, Benjamin, was made a clockmaker to King George III in the late 18th century. Father and son were both known for making repeater movements and were equally expert in their craft.

The 18 with crown over mark was authorised as standard in 1796, and replaced the lion mark. The small letter 'a' was used in the year 1816 confirming that this piece is of George III period.

Having gone crazy on clocks a few years ago, and having quite a few about the house, a friend suggested that some of them might be quite valuable. Most were bought because they attracted me and the price was reasonable, but I do not know a great deal about the technicalities.

Could this clock be dated? It has a black case which stands 16 inches high, and the name on it is Rich'd Gregg, London. It has a brass face, with a strike-silent movement and a window for the date. The back of the clock is very nicely engraved and this is what attracted me to it in the first place. Is it possible to date this clock?

An 18th century bracket clock in an ebonised case

You seem to have collected for the best possible reason — that of being attracted to and liking the things you have bought. This is the surest way to experience enjoyment in possession — thoughts of investment were far from your mind and you have not been dictated to by fashion.

You have a quality timepiece in this clock, which can be termed bracket or table. Its maker, Richard Gregg, is recorded as working at Brentford on the outskirts of London in 1738. He moved into the city to work in St. James Street about 1742. He was a master craftsman who was appointed watchmaker to the King, and keeper of the Palace clocks.

The case is ebonised and has what is known as a basket top, with robust brass handle, which allows the clock to be carried from room to room. This was a not uncommon practice in the period, when clocks were quite expensive and few people could afford one in every room. The case is quite plain, enhanced by an attractive brass dial and spandrels featuring vases of fruit and scrollwork. The name spandrel is given to the attractive brass and gilt pieces applied to the angles edging the numeral ring. The arched dial became popular in the early 18th century. Previously, dials were square.

Good quality early portable clocks like this were usually adorned with an engraved back plate, often visible through a glazed back door, no doubt because they were mainly placed on a table and a pleasant all-round vision was required. Clocks, fixed with back to the wall, like longcases, invariably had a plain brass back plate.

Of course, a well engraved back does enhance the value and stamps a quality label on the clock. This clock with additional dials, date and bob apertures, is without doubt, one of your good buys which has become a fine investment. Dating in the first half of the 18th century, it is well in the four figure bracket and a worthwhile asset to any collector.

We are quite fond of antique pieces and our parents have given us an antique wall clock. The case is japanned with an oriental motif in gold. The numeral ring is also gilded. The maker seems to be Marke Hawkins. We are told it is 'an Act of Parliament clock'. How did these clocks get that name?

A mural or tavern clock c. 1725

Is it Antique?

It would be better to refer to this timepiece as a wall, mural, or tavern clock. The maker, Marke Hawkins, worked as a watch and clock-maker at Bury St. Edmunds in Suffolk, in the early 18th century and the piece would date circa 1725. 'Act of Parliament' is a nomenclature widely used to embrace all the wooden faced wall clocks, which were used in the kitchens of larger houses, inns, government offices and places where the public gathered. The clocks, were generally driven by a single weight, the case being too small to house the extra striking weight. Sometimes there was a small weight to operate the second hand. These clocks are robust and usually very good timekeepers. The Act which has led to some mis-naming in a general term, was instituted long after most of the clocks were made. It came on the Statute Book in 1797 as part of the Finance Act of William Pitt, which put an annual tax on timepieces.

However, it did prove very difficult to collect this tax, and was rescinded, after less than a year in operation.

Early examples of these clocks are sought after by collectors and always make a respectable price at auction.

We have owned a clock for a long time but feel there is something not quite right about it. The case has rather a lot of carving, some of it not too well done. The door is inlaid with a Persian Tree of Life design and the base is carved with quarter fans and a large diamond with a flower in the centre. The dial is brass with a silver painted numeral ring, the figures seem to have been repainted. It has a seconds dial but no hand and there does not appear to be a fitment for one. There is no maker's name anywhere on the clock. Do you think the clock has been made up?

A 19th century longcase clock

The case sounds to be 19th century and it does look a bit overdone, as if something which started as an idea developed into an experiment with wood, and whoever did it got carried away. I do not think there is much doubt that you have a married piece, case, movement and dial. There was probably a maker's name on the dial originally and this has been buffed off during the process of cleaning up and repainting. This situation is not new; it is not unusual to find a longcase clock which has been 'made up'. When paying good money for a clock it is necessary to ensure that this situation does not exist, for a clock to hold its value it should be, in the main, original. Rebushing is sometimes an essential repair and case feet have to be restored. Good restoration is acceptable in the case of clocks as in other things.

Can you date a very nice bracket clock in our possession? It is 20½ inches high and 11½ inches wide. The case is veneered with figured mahogany. It has a brass face with silver ring and strike silent dial. The corners of the face and the arch are decorated with added gilt pieces. There are four gilt urns, one at each corner on the top, which is shaped and has a large brass handle. The movement is barrel type and can be seen through the windows in each side of the case. The back door is arched and glazed, through which the most beautifully engraved back can be seen. Near the bottom of the case there is a carved wood acorn and cup attached to a cord; when this is pulled the strike repeats. The clock stands on brass feet, and was made by Hyland, London.

An 18th century bracket clock in a mahogany case

A very nice and quite valuable clock, obviously with an English fuseé movement and repeater action. The bell top design has a beautiful line, enhanced by the urn flame top finials. The spandrels, as they are called, in the more rococo style with 'C' scrolls, meandering leaves and flower heads, seem to have replaced the cherub heads which were used from about 1670 until circa 1750. Clocks with all-round view were intended for table display rather than bracket. This style had a substantial handle to enable them to be carried with safety from room to room. Clocks were very expensive in the 18th century and only the very wealthy possessed more than one. The engraved backplates are works of art and it does seem a pity that, more often than not, they are against a wall and are seldom seen. This clock was made in the second half of the 18th century; dates circa 1780.

My grandfather went to sea as a boy and eventually captained his own ship out of Liverpool. The family still have two of his seagoing pieces. One is a clock in a mahogany box, made by John Poole of London. The other piece, also in a box, is an instrument for measuring distance. It is made in black wood with an ivory scale. Are these of any particular value today?

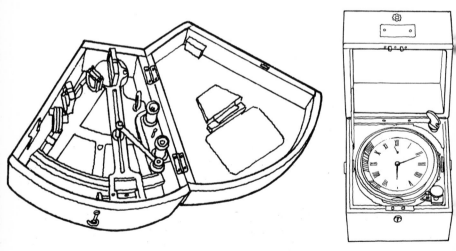

Left, *an octant in a mahogany case.* Right, *a ship's chronometer*

Many instruments were required by a Master mariner as an aid to navigation, and quite important among them was the marine chronometer. Accurate time keeping at sea is important but no ordinary clock could stand up to the conditions. Chronometers were specialist made and had many features. The movement is mounted in gimbals which suspends and keeps it in the horizontal position, no matter how rough the weather. The key is always kept in its place within the case in the top right hand corner, and there is a dial which indicates when rewinding is necessary, for the chronometer must never be allowed to stop. It is the most accurate timepiece ever devised, specially made to compensate for changes in temperature which cause metal to expand or contract.

The movement is controlled by a fuseé. This prevents any deviation when the spring is running down, the same tension is maintained throughout. The marine chronometer is claimed as a British invention by John Harrison, who produced it in 1736. By 1761 tests had been carried out at sea and in that year, one of the chronometers had crossed the Atlantic to Jamaica and back with no appreciable difference of time. However the principle was known earlier and seems to have sprung from that great genius Leonardo Da Vinci who had a fuseé among his drawings. Table clocks were made on the Continent as early as the 17th century using the principle, but it was not applied to marine clocks.

Simply explained, the spring is contained within a barrel to which a gut line or a chain is attached, this passes to the fuseé which is of conical shape and acts as a pulley. On winding, the line is pulled from the spring barrel, causing the spring to tension. As the spring unwinds, the line travels from the narrow end of the fuseé through the graduations, thus the tension is completely uniform throughout the complete run of the spring. The whole thing is easily seen in an early 19th century pocket watch. John Poole was working in London circa 1800 and chronometers from this period are collectors' items and value will certainly run well into three figures.

The other boxed instrument is known as an octant, descended like the sextant, from the earlier Hadley Quadrant. The frame extends one eighth of a circle, hence its name. The instrument measures solar altitude by reflection, which is read off on the scale arc with the aid of a vernier, a sliding scale which sub-divides the smallest divisions against which it slides for accurate reading. All a bit technical for us landlubbers, but a very necessary part of a mariner's everyday life at sea. Octant frames are invariably made in ebony or mahogany. Early octants have the scale made in boxwood, later examples are in ivory. Your example is 19th century and it does have a value running into three figures. With two good examples, you have the basis for a collection of scientific instruments concerned with the sea. There are quite a number for your selection.

Banjo barometers have been given their name because of the shape. Is there a special name for a long narrow barometer in a mahogany case? The weather scale is at the top, enclosed by a glass door. The mercury tube runs the whole length into a round shape at the base.

The barometer is 38 inches long and was made by Jho. Conti, Holborn Hill, London.

A mahogany stick barometer

Barometers are often named after their shapes. 'Signal' and 'wheel' barometers are other examples of this. The one in question is called a 'stick' because of its long and narrow shape. This style was the earliest used domestic barometer in Britain and Sir Samuel Morland, master of mechanics to King Charles II was concerned with its evolvement. It works by the cistern method, a long glass tube filled with mercury, the open end placed in a cistern of mercury at the base. Atmospheric pressure causes the mercury to move in the tube and register against the scale provided. A case was required for such a fragile piece, and early ones were made in ebony, walnut, and sometimes olivewood. Mahogany came on the scene in the 18th century, and as a popular furnishing wood it necessarily followed that barometer cases were made in this wood. The cases, generally made by clock case makers, have some of the characteristics of the longcase. This example has the architectural pediment often seen on clocks. The moulded roundel at the base covers the cistern.

English barometer cases of the 18th century are mainly undecorated, unlike the French pieces which can be quite elaborate with ormolu mounts and sometimes Sevres porcelain plaques. There are some English exceptions, particularly when wholly produced by clock-makers. This barometer by a well known maker dates circa 1800 and although unadorned will look attractive on a plain wall.

The photograph is of an unusual barometer. Can you tell us something about it?

Admiral Fitzroy's barometer

This instrument is known as 'Admiral Fitzroy's barometer', for the reason that he was the inventor.

Robert Fitzroy was born in 1805 into a noble family. His father was a Lord and his grandfather a Duke. He entered the Royal Naval College in London as a young man and served with the Royal Navy. He commanded the *Beagle*, with Darwin aboard, on the expedition to survey the South American coast.

Later, Fitzroy was appointed Governor of New Zealand, and became a Vice Admiral in 1863.

He is especially remembered for his invention of this type of barometer which could be mass produced and cheaper than anything else available. To use the instrument properly, and it is quite an accurate forecaster, the instructions printed on the face require to be carefully followed. These are not difficult to follow, (i.e., if the mercury rises very high suddenly, fine weather will not last long). In very hot weather the fall of the mercury denotes thunder, sudden fall indicates high winds. A fall when the thermometer is low denotes snow or rain, etc. It is not sufficient to set the pointers; sea level requires a calculation, and other factors explained on the face have to be considered.

This is decorative, as well as being a collectors' item.

10   Pottery and Porcelain

A pair of vases with dished covers have come into our possession. They are 12 inches high and have all the hallmarks of Derby in colouring and decoration. They are of beautiful quality. Could they be Derby and about what date?

A pair of mid 19th century ice pails

The original Derby factory earned a Royal Warrant from George III. In spite of this I have always felt that the early ware should be referred to as 'Derby'. Perhaps I should explain why.

A Company was formed in 1876 named Derby Crown Porcelain Company. After it had received a Royal Warrant from Queen Victoria, it became known as the Royal Crown Derby Porcelain Company, hence the term Crown Derby. This factory was situated at Osmaston Road, Derby. The original Derby factory continued at King Street and it was not until years later that it was absorbed into the Royal Crown Derby establishment. I think this pair of vases, (which are in fact ice pails), are a product made around the mid 19th century, at a time when the King Street works was in the hands of Stevenson and Hancock.

Had there been a mark, it would have been in the style of the crossed swords with three dots each side, initials S.H., the imperial crown and Derby D. (The King Street works was carried on by Samson Hancock after the death of Stevenson in 1866. The initials S.H. were his own, so he continued to use the mark).

Derby always employed very capable artists. Potting and decoration was superb throughout the whole period. William Billingsley could probably be termed the father of them all. He was an apprentice under William Duesbury and became one of the finest decorators. He later worked for other factories including Worcester. He did start a factory of his own at Nantgarw in Wales, but did not meet with any great success. He was responsible for the teaching of many apprentices in the art of decoration. After much wandering Billingsley finally went to work at Coalport and died in 1828.

Can you classify a blue and white jug in quite fine porcelain? It has a mask on the spout and is decorated with trees in landscale with cartouche. The base is marked with what looks to be a quarter moon.

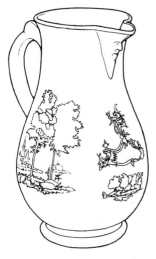

A first period Worcester ale or cider jug

It may seem strange for a Doctor of Medicine to set up a china works. Dr Wall did just that, within the walls of an old Mansion House on the banks of the River Severn in 1751. A man of many talents, he was also a painter of some merit and his knowledge of chemistry was extensive. It was this knowledge which he used in the manufacture of porcelain. Dr Wall, in partnership with several others, set up the Worcester Porcelain Works. The paste was compact and soft, decorated by hand and transfer printed. Early marks were used in the form of a crescent, usually in outline on painted pieces and filled in on transfer ware. The factory produced much in the way of useful ware.

Your jug is a cider or ale jug from what is known as first period Worcester. Sometimes these are printed with a beverage name. It is a collectors' piece, so look after it. Dr Wall died in 1776.

Worcester has a long history in the making of good quality porcelain and has been well documented. There is much of interest in the reference works for the would-be collector.

I was wondering how the Chinese garden seat got its name, for it is difficult to think that these beautiful objects were kept outside. We have one which is gaily coloured, decorated with flowers and a large central conversational piece showing a group of figures on terraced steps. It would be interesting to know the history of these seats?

A Canton cool seat

The Chinese name for the seats is 'liang tun' which means cool seat. The climate in China can be extreme in both degrees. These seats were used in the summer period, placed outside on the terraces and in the confetti gardens of the summer palaces used by the Mandarins and Peking dignitaries. The scene on your piece depicts a terrace composition, with a Mandarin surrounded by his attendants.

The shape of the seats is interesting and leads one to think that they were inspired by the drum. Most have a band of studs near the top and bottom, which resembles the assembly of that instrument. In early examples of seats, the studs are quite pronounced.

They seem to have evolved during the Ming period and made in blue and white. Examples show open work bodies which must have been a nightmare to the potter, for the contractions and expansions which occur during firing could cause a collapse in such a design.

The potters moved on to the closed bodies, no doubt to avoid the heavy punishments meted out in the event of too much wastage. The open seats were of course so much cooler, allowing the breeze to pass right through. By the K'ang Hsi period the seats had become more elongated and decorated in several colours with traditional scenes and legendary characters. The later Canton decorated seats have many enamel colours. Early cool seats are mostly in museums and private collections and rarely come on the market.

Can you possibly date a very attractive plate made by Minton? The colours are grey and white, the white areas raised in relief. It also has a small mark which looks like a cross within a square, it that helps at all.

A Minton plate

This Minton ware is known as 'Paté sur Paté', translated from the French 'paste on paste', quite an appropriate name for that is how it is created. The ground colour plate is fashioned first, then a creamy mixture of paste is brushed on coat by coat where the pattern is desired to form a relief. The skill of the artist then comes into play. He scrapes the paste to the required thickness and carves it with much care into desired design. The piece is given another firing and is ready to receive the glaze. A final firing completes as you see, a beautiful result.

The process, paste on paste, was used by Chinese potters long before it came to Europe. It is surprising how long it took Europeans to fathom the mysteries of the art of Chinese potting, which had been used for hundreds of years! The secrets were well kept, no doubt due to the fact that the kilns were controlled by the emperors, and severe punishments were meted out to transgressors. There is an interesting story that when a potter produced some inferior work, he was hurled into his own kiln. It is said that when the pieces of pot were removed afterwards, it was of the finest and the potter was thus immortalised. It could have been the first discovery that bone ash improved the porcelain.

The Minton factory always employed the finest artists and one who came from Sevres, Marc L. Solon, was much concerned in the making of paté sur paté pieces and items signed by him are much sought after. Minton, over a long period, used a system of date marking with small impressed devices, symmetricals, horseshoes, crowns, knots, rising sun and many others too numerous to mention. They have all been documented in works of reference.

Your plate has the cypher for the year 1884 and a collection of these very attractive and artistic pieces is well worthwhile.

Among our collection of small ornaments, we have what are termed 'fairings'. One is quite a humorous piece with the caption 'Last into bed put out the light'. It shows a man and woman getting into a half tester bed, with a candle on a table at the foot. Are these pieces very old?

An example of a Victorian fairing

'Fairings' is the general name given to all sorts of small ornaments from the Victorian and Edwardian period, mainly figure groups and china boxes. Many had some sort of caption, (often with an under-tone), which the Victorians would have considered a bit naughty. A great number of these pieces were made from about 1860 onwards. The Conta and Boehme factory at Possneck, Saxony is probably the originator. There was quite a demand for these little pieces of inexpensive nonsense, and other factories soon saw the possibilities and got 'into the act'. Later, the Japanese also went into mass production. Up to the first world war there was a tremendous sale at seaside gift shops, and pieces were used as prizes by the showmen at fair grounds.

The English captions were no doubt sent from this country by firms ordering quantities of the ware. Serious collectors, (and there are a number), favour factory named and numbered pieces and there are items which are considered rare. There is quite a variation in quality, some being positively crude.

For my own part, I have not been able to find much enthusiasm for fairings and have often been surprised at the prices obtained at auction. Obviously some people hold them in high regard, and why not, if they find pleasure in collecting them? I admit that an arranged cabinet display can look quite attractive.

Can you define the country of origin of a boat shaped dessert dish? It is 17 inches long and 8½ inches wide. The colour of the paste is creamy white. The dish has an oval base well hollowed and shows three wavy lines in blue. The edges are decorated in high quality gilt and there is a melon and other fruit painted in the bowl and a smaller group on the outside. The painting is obviously by hand. Hair crazing can be seen in the glaze.

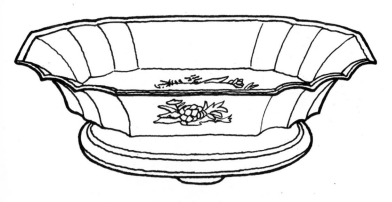

A Copenhagen dessert dish

This sounds like a very nice dessert dish, no doubt once part of a service, from the Copenhagen factory which was established 1772 by a chemist named Muller.

The factory produced hard paste porcelain, with a high percentage of crystalline feldspar, combined with fine china clay. The paste produces the very attractive limpid white. Decorative colours are subdued and simple, blues, greys, greens, browns and gilt. The blue wavy lines, three in all, represent the Great and Little Belts and the Sound. They do not always represent an early piece, but from what you have indicated about the quality of the decoration, this piece has been around a long time and dates circa 1800. It is considered a desirable collectors' piece.

Copenhagen produces fine ornamental pieces, in addition to useful ware. Collections of figures, birds, fish and other subjects are well worth while and are found in biscuit and subdued tints. Items marked B & G are products from the Bing and Gröndhall factory which started in 1858.

We have a part dessert service which is always admired by visitors. It is beautifully decorated with berries, fruits, hanging lamps and flower panels on a pure white porcelain. The tureen and cover are 7 inches in diameter and have scallop shell handles. There are four scallop shell dishes and several plates. They all have centre pieces decorated with different groups of seashells. The borders are deep blue. We would like to know when it was made and if it is considered a collector's item.

Left, *a Chamberlain Worcester dish.* Right, *a Chamberlain Worcester tureen and stand*

From the decoration, and looking at the photographs, I think your part dessert can be considered a fine collection of porcelain. It looks like the product of Chamberlain, Worcester. Robert Chamberlain first learned his trade at the old Worcester Company. In about the year 1789 he started in Worcester and, helped by his brother, took on decoration work for other factories. A few years later they were joined with the Flight and Barr Company and became known as Chamberlain and Company. It is not always realised that there were a number of factories in Worcester apart from the one established by Dr Wall. All. these manufacturers made fine pieces.

The dessert service dates early 19th century. I do not know exactly how many pieces you have but any one piece is a collector's item. This must have been a magnificent service when complete and is a prime example of the potters' and decorators' skill.

A figure of a man on rocky stump base, seems to be playing a drum. The colours are fairly bright and there are traces of what might have been gilding. There are no potter's marks but a number of imperfections similar to those seen on Plymouth ware. Could the piece have been made there?

A Plymouth/Longton Hall figure

The Plymouth factory was founded by a John Cooksworthy, a west countryman born at Kingsbridge, Devon in 1705. It is perhaps to him that the long and still continuing production in the Cornish china clay industry can be attributed. It is said that he discovered for Britain the secret of porcelain known for centuries by the Chinese and latterly at Meissen. Cooksworthy was a chemist, a profession he learned in London before returning to set up business in Devon.

Cooksworthy spent a great deal of time in Cornwall and it was there that the materials for the porcelain process were discovered (whether by accident or design, it is difficult to say). His enquiring mind may have perhaps been attracted to the milky whiteness of a stream, who knows? However, he did find the necessary ingredients, kaolin and petunste. We do not know when his experiments started. The first date to give the lead was 1768, when a patent was taken out in conjunction with the then Lord Camelford, on whose land the discovery was made, and the production of true porcelain began.

The factory produced much useful ware as well as decorative pieces. Cooksworthy was a better chemist than a potter and firing faults occurred, leaving tiny black sooty spots and other imperfections. Before opening at Plymouth, Cooksworthy joined Richard Champion at Bristol. About 1773 John Cooksworthy retired from business and the patent for the making of porcelain became the property of the Bristol factory.

Figures similar to that you describe were made at Plymouth but during the period, moulds and even decorators moved about quite a bit and pieces in similar vein were made at Longton Hall, where imperfections in firing also existed.

It has been recorded that moulds from Longton Hall were used at Plymouth. Specimens rarely show a factory mark, but items from both Longton Hall and Plymouth are quite rare and are prized among collectors.

I enjoy going to sales and buying odd pieces of china. One day, I bought a box lot, among which was a two handled vase with a damaged base. The colours are quite bright with blues, reds and giltwork. It stands 12 inches high. There was a cracked saucer in the same lot which is of similar colour and is marked Crown Derby. Could vase be Derby and is it possible to get it repaired?

A Derby vase

It is surprising sometimes what can be found in job lots. Dealers are known to clear out their broken and unrequired stock from time to time and put it in a sale for what it will fetch. Not long ago I saw such a box lot in auction; it consisted of several badly damaged figures. The lady who bought the lot told me that she had arranged to attend a course to learn china repairing and was required to take along any broken pieces she had, in order to carry out repairs as a test at the end of tuition. I often wonder how she got on and if she managed to restore the pieces to a resemblance of their former brilliance. If the vase is of similar shape and pattern to the illustration you could well have a Derby piece. If it happened to have a shell motif in the centre panel it would leave little doubt. China and porcelain can be repaired using the expertise of the professional. There are good restorers available but you have to be prepared to often wait some time before they can complete your work. It is as well to remember with regard to restoration that you get what you pay for. A cheap job can be a complete waste of money, apart from the possibility of ruining the piece for all time.

Would a commemorative shaving mug made for King Edward VIII coronation be of extra special value, as the King was never crowned?

A commemorative shaving mug for Edward VIII's coronation

As with other national events, British potteries went into high production to commemorate the coronation of Edward VIII. Commemorations of a non-event, although taking their place in collections, cannot be considered to have any special value above others.

This piece would better hold its place among a collection of shaving mugs. These do not sound terribly exciting, but there are some quite varied and attractive ones. These pots are fast disappearing from use and becoming relics of the past, as are the cut-throat razor with which they were associated.

Modern methods of shaving have dispensed with the shaped mug specially made for the purpose, so a collection of a few of the nicer ones would not go amiss.

After being given a few pieces I have become attracted to the idea of making a collection of commemorative pottery. Knowing little about the subject, it would be interesting to know if such a venture would be worthwhile for a person of moderate means?

Commemorative plates for Edward VII and Queen Alexandra's coronation

All types of pottery commemoratives were generally produced in quite large quantities. They were a purely commercial venture to take advantage of a short period of mass sale in connection with events of national importance. Commemoratives speak for themselves with their pictures and inscriptions. It is advisable to acquire some knowledge in order to be able to distinguish quality. Many pieces were quite poor in execution, while others made by premier potteries, show the same good quality of their normal ware. Starting now as you are, it will indeed be good fortune to come across early pieces within your reach, but it does happen and much of the joy in collecting, is the hunt for a bargain. The quest can take you to interesting places which you might not otherwise visit.

Rare items of course do command a price often beyond the reach of the small collector, but one must live with the. consolation that all things gather rarity with the passage of time. The 1977 Jubilee of Queen Elizabeth II produced a vast quantity. The collector can find some attractive pieces if he is choosy and concentrates on quality.

Working backwards to coronations and other jubilees, the collection will grow. In the early 19th century, national figures, like Nelson and Wellington, were commemorated in a very big way, and some of these will probably be the earliest available to you. 18th century pieces are very rare and mostly in the hands of museums or in private collections. At least you can and should, visit and view a collection whenever you have the opportunity.

Commemoratives take many forms but mostly, mugs, jugs, teapots, bowls and plates. Pieces with factory marks are of added historical interest. Doulton spirit flasks and other pieces in salt glaze should not be overlooked. The Reform Law series of the William IV period and the later General Gordon and Stanley commemoratives were made in quantity and could still be available to you. Railway commemoratives are rare but worth searching for. It is as well to remember that not all of the ware is coloured. There are a large number of black and white examples. The field is wide and a good collection properly displayed is a joy to view.

Are brownware Doulton jugs worth collecting? We have one with a silver band round the top, date letter mark 'h' for 1904. The base is marked Royal Doulton, England, with lion surmount.

A Doulton salt glaze jug with a silver rim

Brown salt glaze ware pieces were mainly utilitarian. Some, like drain pipes, and water coolers, were not very exciting. It is easy to manufacture, requiring only one firing, and the glaze is introduced by adding salt to the kiln. Doulton's also produced salt glaze in art form; the ware could be decorated while still in clay state. The ale jugs were so much more attractive with the relief decoration, and the decorators at Lambeth were given a fairly free hand so that even a mundane brown utilitarian article became something of a work of art. Brownware from the Lambeth factory does offer a fair range to the collector and is worth acquiring. Items with silver mounts (from jugs down to small lucifer pots) could be quite interesting, and would make an attractive display. There are Toby jugs, bust figures of statesmen, Queen Victoria, jubilee models, Admiral Nelson's centenary, Great War leaders, Marshall Foch, Admiral Beatty, and sporting characters like the famous racing jocky Archer. There is no end to it really; you decide what you want and seek it out. Lambeth is of course now closed, which makes it even more interesting and worthwhile to collect the work which came from that factory.

Is it possible to attribute a two-handled pedestal vase to any particular factory? The background colour is blue. It has a white panel back and front surrounded by gold scrollwork, within which there are hand painted flowers comprising clematis, polyanthus, tulips, sunflowers and convolvulus. The handles are scrolled leaves with gold edges. It is 10 inches high. There is a mark on the base which looks like a rose.

From the description this sounds like a vase from the Coalport factory; a rose was used as a mark about the year 1810. The factory was established by John Rose about 1785. It was well established by the late nineties and in 1799 took over the Caughly factory and this eventually moved to Coalport. The empire was expanded later with the purchase of Swansea and Nantgarw in 1820 and 1828. It is interesting that quite a number of early British factories changed hands after only a short time in production. Unlike some of the continental factories, British factories did not enjoy royal patronage until late in the day.

Porcelain was expensive to manufacture and several factories found themselves in difficulty and unable to pay their way. Porcelain was not for the masses until very much later. Various marks are found on Coalport, including copies of the Dresden crossed swords, Sevres cypher, and Chelsea anchor. A mark incorporating CSN about 1830 represents Caughly, Swansea and Nantgarw amalgamation. Coalport offers a wide range to the collector and is not too difficult to find.

Can you define the factory and age of a porcelain figure which is 16 inches tall? The costume is in 18th century style comprising a brown tricorn hat with a reddish pink ostrich feather, pale blue frock coat, grey breeches, white stockings, pink garters and shoes. The base is in rococo style with stump support. There is a 'D' mark crossed with two lines in blue and impressed numbers which look like 857.

A porcelain figure musician

The 'D' mark was used by the Vienna factory originally established in 1718 by a Dutchman named Du Pasquier. He was assisted by a man named Stenzel whom he persuaded to leave Meissen and work with him at Vienna. The factory was not too successful, and by the mid 18th century it had been taken over by the state. It prospered for a few years then declined, but picked up again near the end of the century as a result of employing first class artists and designers. Flaxman, (who was also associated with Wedgwood), was among them. The early 19th century saw another decline, with the loss of substantial sums of money for the state, which eventually sold up in 1864. Vienna style ware continued to be produced but of indifferent quality, catering for the cheaper end of the market. In the 19th century, when the original Vienna factory was at work, it was a practice to impress the last three numbers of the year on the base. 857 would indicate the year 1857. It must be added that the 'D' mark in blue has been used in much later productions, by minor factories, imitating the Vienna ware.

We understand that the mark showing a crescent in blue was used on early Worcester, and feel that an oval bowl 12 inches long with open work border, could be from that factory. It is blue and white with a central decoration of flowers and leafy branches. These do not appear to be hand painted; would transfers have been used on early pieces?

A first period Worcester dish

You are quite correct in your understanding about the mark; it is associated with early pieces. Both open and closed crescent in under-glaze blue was used. Transfer printing was used in the first, or Dr Wall period, as it is sometimes called. For a long time blue and white ware was pretty well ignored, and not many years ago, I heard people saying 'Oh, it's blue and white, not worth a lot', and I suppose at the time they were right for none seemed very keen. Worcester produced useful ware on a large scale and there must still be plenty to be discovered by the collector. The range is wide, and small items like eyebaths, tobacco stoppers, sauce boats, tea bowls, dishes, and believe it or not, chamber pots, often appear where least expected. Junk box lots in the smaller auctions are always worth looking through.

Worcester figures are rare but do appear from time to time. Ware with armorials are prized, as are the rare red scale grounds, copied from the Chinese. The Worcester name continues and the more modern Royal Worcester, is well worth consideration. Limited editions are not a bad idea, as they become collectors' items in no time at all and a beginner would be wise to collect them.

We have a pottery garden seat which we understand is Chinese. The decoration is in Oriental style, with flowering cherry branches, chrysanthemums and symbols. The top and bottom borders are a lightish brown; there are two bands of painted studs. The colours are not very bright and fairly flat. There are no marks on the piece; what do you think about it?

A Japanese pottery garden seat

The fact that you are enquiring perhaps indicates that you have a little doubt in your mind. Not all cool seats were made in China. The fact that this one is in pottery suggests that it was not made in China. The flowering prunus decoration, chrysanthemums which are the emblem of the Empress, and Suwo type symbols, are the signs that it was made in Japan. The Japanese made them specifically for export to the European market, particularly in the late 19th century. The pottery seats of Japanese origin do not have the same care in potting and decoration as their Chinese counterparts in porcelain. And, although it may seem strange, garden cool seats were also reproduced in the Staffordshire potteries! However, even the late pottery pieces can be attractive and although not having the greater value of Chinese porcelain ones, can find a place in the decorative scheme within the home, for none would be placed in the garden these days. I have seen them used as occasional tables and as a stand for an oriental vase or bronze.

Can you say if a Doulton bottle type vase is antique? It has a deep blue background with Persian type decoration in grey and brown glaze. It stands 15 inches high and the mark on the base, Doulton, Lambeth, England, four joined capital D's in circle. Are Doulton Lambeth pieces worth collecting?

The quick answer to the first question is 'No', to the second 'Yes', but we cannot leave it at that. The beginnings for Doulton were quite small. John Doulton, in company with two other men, set up in a small pot yard at Vauxhall Walk, Lambeth, London, in 1815. John, who had served his apprenticeship with Dwights of Fulham, had learned the business well and was expert at the potter's wheel; he could throw a pot with the best of them. The factory became known as

Doulton and Watts. The partners faced a considerable up hill struggle for survival. After about three years the establishment had acquired sufficient orders to warrant another kiln. Spirit flasks in various forms were a popular production and jugs in the likeness of Nelson, Napoleon, Wellington and others were popular and sold in vast numbers in the 1820's.

After 1830, more kilns were added and the factory branched out with building materials. Chimney pots, ridge tiles and other terra cotta pieces were made. John's son Henry, born in 1820, joined the firm in 1835 and even the boss's son had to serve his apprenticeship. Like his father, Henry became expert at the wheel. On his twenty-first birthday he potted what was said to be the largest pot in the world, by way of celebration. This pot, which could hold three hundred gallons, was exhibited at Lambeth for many years. Henry was a driving force, and the factory turned out massive quantities of tiles and building materials. Not many London buildings in the period failed to display some ornamentation made by Doultons.

The Great Exhibition in Hyde Park, London, in 1851, was used to exhibit Doulton ware, which received first class awards. Hundreds of commendations have been won since then. John Doulton died in 1873 leaving Henry to carry on. By this time he had become interested in the Arts and formed an association with a John Sparks of the Lambeth School of Art. Students were encouraged to design for the factory, and given a fairly free hand to create some quite artisic pieces. Many of these remain to be admired today. A steady stream of art students passed through the factory including George Tinworth, members of the now well-known Barlow family and others. They were all allowed to mark their work, so they can be identified.

The factory produced a great range of pieces for the collector but they seem to have been sadly neglected between and after the wars. Those who saw the possibility early now not only have visual benefit, but investment of considerable growth. Doulton commemoratives and other decorative wares are legion; there is still scope for the beginner to form a reasonable collection which will prove well worthwhile.

The vase in question is circa 1904 but, as I said, is not yet antique. Nevertheless, it is a collector's item. It may help to add that any piece where the word 'England' is in the mark, will date later than 1891. This country of origin mark was used to comply with the American Customs laws at that time, known as the McKinley Tariff Act. The added words 'made in' appeared in the 1920's — a note which can be helpful in determining a period.

We have a very interesting piece of blue and white pottery. It is in the form of a fisherman's head wearing a sou'wester hat. The top of the hat forms a lid. It is 5 inches high and marked Delft on the base; also a small device and a letter 'F'. Is it very old?

A late 19th century Delft tobacco jar

Delf is the general name given to tin enamelled ware no matter where it was made. Delft, the ancient town in Holland, has been associated with the manufacture of delf over a long period. The ware has been made there for well over three hundred years. It is interesting that the early craftsmen in Delft were organised into a very powerful body known as the Guild of St Luc, which laid down very strict rules, with heavy penalties for any breach of them. There was a proving period for membership and apprentices were required to pass a test in their given trade. Potters were included and were required to submit a mark to be registered. No one could work without being a member of the Guild — it was a craft closed shop. Thanks to the strict control of mark registration, Dutch potters can be identified. The Delft tobacco jar is quite interesting but not an early piece, being made by the late 19th century faience factory of Thoovt and Labouchere. This factory has produced many reproductions of early Delft ware, not with any attempt to fake or deceive, but purely as a tribute to the earlier potters.

Delft pieces from the early 17th century, bear quite characteristic marks with initials and or symbols. For instance, the three bells in pyramid indicating the De Drie Klokken factory established by Simon Mesch in 1671. Most of the factories had romantic names. When translated from the Dutch some read, Three Porcelain Bottles, The Rose, The Golden Flower Pot, The Star and so on. If you like blue and white ware, the delf from Delft offers a wide choice. Early pieces often show a little damage; the base pottery is quite soft and the tin glaze very hard so a slight knock can cause the glaze to fly off, particularly on rims. Even so, much has survived intact. The modern pieces also have their attraction decorated with windmill landscapes and other Dutch scenes.

It would be interesting to know about a mark on a decorated sauceboat. It is triangular in shape, with a circle at the top containing the Roman numeral IV. The angles are lined off, having letters and figures. The letters 'Rd' are in the central position.

This is a registration mark used in the 19th century, and indicates that the design had been registered at the Patent Office. The mark was usually impressed for the pattern and printed for the decoration. Items so marked prevented competitors from copying for three years, thus allowing the originator to exploit the piece. The device was used in this form from 1842 to 1883. From the letters and numbers it is possible to near date the item on which it appears. From 1842 to 1867 the letter seen under the Roman numeral indicated the year, the letter on the left the month, the number on the right the day. The figure at the bottom, a manufacturer's code.

From 1868 the sequence changed; the figure at the top indicating the day, the letter at the bottom the month, the letter at the right the year, manufacturer's code on the left. This device was also used for other materials; each indicated by the Roman numeral at the crest; I for metal objects, II for wood, III for glass. The complete code guide can be found in reference works which deal with china marks. The table is quite simple to follow and makes dating easy.

We have a small sauce boat in blue and white pottery which is thought to be quite old. In what period were these made without handles?

A pap boat or baby feeder

Although these small pieces resemble sauceboats and may well have been used as such at some time, they are really 'pap boats'. The design has been around for a very long time. They were in use as early as the 16th century in this country. Some are made in silver.

Porcelain and pottery pap boats were produced on quite a large scale and offer a good selection of decorative designs to the collector who might also include babies feeding bottles to go with them.

Pap boats were baby feeders usually containing a mixture of bread and water perhaps laced with ale or wine. Several factories produced for this lucrative market on a mass production scale. Examples from Minton, Wedgwood, Davenport and Spode can be found. Infants seem not to have been fed with milk from animals in earlier days. The habit of feeding may well have changed with the advent of the 'bubbly pot' in the late 18th century, which looked like a covered mug with a watering-can spout. This was followed by the bottle feeder which was filled from the top, often termed 'submarine' because of the resemblance in shape to that vessel. Perhaps you may now feel that you would like to start a collection of these interesting items.

We have a large pair of Chinese vases both with lids. They are 30 inches high. The colours are quite beautiful mainly in deep blue and red with some gilding. They do not have any china marks on the base. The ground colour is off white, with a greyish tinge. They are not damaged in any way. Are they very old?

A late 19th century Japanese vase with cover

These are oriental vases, not Chinese but Japanese. This type of decorated ware is given the general name 'Imari' but were made at kilns in the Arita district. The name is derived from the port of Imari from where they were shipped. Imari is a traditional export ware for the European market and Dutch traders were doing quite a lot of business with Imari ware as early as the 17th century. Early ware was made in a fairly rough paste. The decoration colours were not very pure and the glaze left much to be desired. The 18th century European demand was for something better, so the potting and decoration was improved. Artists took more care and more traditional Japanese designs were used. Decorations included the chrysanthemum, delicate wistaria tracery, sometimes landscape panels and occasionally figures. Some patterns were copied in Europe and the British Worcester factory produced 'old Japan' in the 18th century. This design has oriental character marks to complete the picture. No doubt many an early Worcester piece has been passed over in the past and thought to be Japanese by the less informed. Imari pattern has probably been the greatest range of any Japanese export ware. It has lasted through the centuries only being disrupted by 19th century internal troubles. Exports suffered but were renewed from about 1870 and still find favour.

Imari ware offers quite a range to the collector who prefers a colourful display. A pair of these floor vases is not easy to find in perfect condition and values have considerably increased over the past few years. They are a bit vulnerable if displayed as they were intended and are best placed on a table for corner display. Yours dates late 19th century and can be prized.

We have one or two pieces of unusual pottery bearing the signature Martin Brothers. One is an amusing bird vase about 8 inches high. The bird's head forms the lid. It has a terrific expression, more like a caricature. We bought this piece at a small shop some years ago and would like to know something about Martin Brothers and the possible date of the vase.

The pieces you have are known as Martin ware, and made by a family who started in Fulham in 1873. Later, in 1878, they expanded to Southall in the county of Middlesex. The work of the four Martin brothers was quite unusual and was sold from their own shop in London. The obvious intention of this studio pottery was to create something different and they succeeded. (Robert Martin was a competent sculptor, having studied at the Royal Academy schools.) They made use of 'Gres-ceramique' (stoneware with ceramic glaze), a material used 200 years before on the continent, which has a durable quality and which was a perfect medium for the type of ware produced. This included bird vases, (sometimes called tobacco jars), jugs, vases, pots, beakers — and I have seen a sundial.

Martinware, not yet antique, (apart from the production of the first three or four years), is worth collecting. It is unique in design and decoration, some of the more bizarre pieces can be termed beautifully ugly. Three of the brothers died within a few years of each other, leaving Robert, who was basically a sculptor, and he found himself unable to carry on. The studio finally closed at the beginning of the First World War. Do try and add to your collection, for you can be assured that each piece acquired will be different in design or decoration. All pieces bear an identification mark and often a date, impressed or incised. Pieces where the mark has Bros. or Brothers are dated after 1882.

Robert Martin died in 1923, thus ending a family of craftsmen who created one of the most exciting studio potteries of the period.

A pottery milk bucket which stands on my kitchen dresser always arouses interest and I wonder if it can be termed a collector's piece as no one seems to have seen another like it. It has a steel liner with a brass cover; the body is decorated with branches of autumn leaves and the words 'New Milk'. There is a mark on the base which says 'Dairy Supply Company, Museum Street, London'. It has scrolled carrying handles and is 12 inches high.

A pottery milk pail

This milk container is a bit of a rarity, and is of the type which was used in small country dairies, and could also be seen standing on a slate cool slab in the larder of a large house. I cannot trace the suppliers at the Museum Street address and do not know if they are still in business. There is a company with a similar sounding name in another part of London but my efforts to contact have not proved fruitful. This piece was probably made in Staffordshire to special order of the dairy suppliers but difficult to date; it might well be 19th century. There is a wide range of paraphernalia connected with the dairy trade and there are interested collectors. This could safely be placed in this category. If you can find one of the metal hook handle measures used in the dairy and by roundsmen before the advent of bottles, the picture would be complete.

We would like to know the date and manufacturer of a pair of vases. They are 8 inches high with white background decorated with gold scrolls and leaves. There are two square panels with baskets of garden flowers, tulips, polyanthus, carnations and chrysanthemums. There is a mark on the base taking the form of crossed letter Ł' Louis cypher with what appears to be a letter B. There is a crown over the top.

Quite often this mark could be taken for that used for a period at the French factory at Sevres. However, this pair of vases is English and made at Derby. The earliest factory of any note recorded at Derby seems to be the Derby Pot Works, about the middle of the 18th century.

Duesbury is the man usually associated with early Derby porcelain. He died in 1776. His son, also named William, succeeded to the business and was assisted in management by a Mr Kean, who had been associated previously with the father. Kean was a fine artist and designer and so was a useful asset to the young Duesbury. Moving quickly on, the factory passed to Robert Bloor about 1815. He rapidly expanded the business and his was the period when your vases were made. This mark, which does resemble the Sevres, was used about 1825 to 1848. So the vases are 19th century Derby. Although not too important, they are quite nice collectors' pieces.

We have a brightly coloured dish 12 inches in diameter; we are told it is Imari. Can you expand on its origin?

The name 'Imari' is the general term used for this Japanese ware and is taken from the port from which it was shipped. The ware is actually made inland in the Arita district. Very early ware was made with dark blue underglaze with some overglaze in red and gold. Designs from this were copied on Delft made in Europe and later by English factories including Derby and Worcester. In later years the colours became more vivid, using multiple colours of blue, red, gold, green, yellow and manganese. The pattern became very crowded, featuring baskets of flowers, sprays, landscapes, animals, birds and the chrysanthemum which is an Emporial emblem. Some Imari pieces bore faked Chinese character marks; in the main they are unmarked. Modern Imari is not well decorated, being done in a somewhat careless manner. 19th century pieces show more care.

There is quite a wide range for the collector comprising square, round and oval dishes, several sizes of plates, large bottle vases, square vases and bowls. All are made for export to the European market and are not styled for home use. Imari is fairly easy to find in shops and frequently comes up at auction. It makes a bright display and is a good complement to a piece of oriental furniture in the home.

An amusing figure has sat on our mantelpiece for many years, and we have often wondered about its age. Made in pottery, he wears a tricorn hat, blue frock coat, yellow waistcoat and pale pink breeches. His arm rests on a circular table at his side and he holds an ale jug and mug. The amusing feature is the peg leg which sticks out before him. The base is slightly hollowed and has a small hole in it. Is it a Staffordshire piece and is it rare?

A Staffordshire figure 'Greenwich Pensioner' c. 1860

You have described a Staffordshire figure, the all embracing name given to the whole range of figure groups made in this style. There is quite a large collector interest and the range is very wide, allowing specialisation in some of the series like boxers and other sportsmen, Royal families and notable people; there are even animal figures and cottages. The ware was made right through the 19th century and produced a pictorial and historical review of the period. Modellers were inspired by events, personalities, even engravings and music covers. Some of the pieces have captions. They were made by various factories and are most difficult to attribute, having no marks to help in positive identification. Potters like William Kent and John Parr of Burslem are known makers. Moulds sometimes changed hands and this makes it even more difficult to identify the maker of a piece.

Some pieces are very rare and command quite high prices. Even in the 19th century, reproductions were made from older moulds. Early pieces were made by pressing clay into a two-, (or more), part mould. Later the slip was poured and when partly set, the liquid centre poured away leaving the hollow interior smooth. The experienced collector who is willing to pay quite high prices, can examine the interior through the hole (left to allow the steam to escape during firing) by using an optical instrument with a roving head and reflector to reproduce an image of the interior.

As in every field there are modern reproductions in some cases with deliberate artificially crackled glaze which has been stained to simulate age. When contemplating a purchase, treat catalogues and price tags which do not stipulate other than Staffordshire with some caution. Modern reproductions should be priced accordingly. With experience, colouring can prove one of the best guides, modern colours are not as soft as early pigments. If you are going to collect in a serious way, a reliable dealer will prove your best friend; there are specialists in the field who stake their names on the pieces they sell. Although you may not have seen this peg leg figure before, it is not considered one of the rare examples. Known as 'Greenwich Pensioner' it was made circa 1860.

Not long ago we bought a Toby jug. The man who sold it to us could not tell us anything about its age. It has a black hat, dark blue coat and yellow breeches; the colours are nice and bright. The base is flat and there are large crazed cracks which have turned brown, which gives us the impression that it is quite old. Can you give any idea about the date it was made?

A Staffordshire Toby jug

If you bought the Toby jug at a shop, then the dealer should have been able to tell you if it was old. From what you say about the flat bottom, bright colours and large cracks with staining, this Toby is suspect. It seems very much as if it has been given an aging treatment. Toby jugs are still being manufactured from 19th century moulds, but the makers in no way attempt to fake them. Reproductions are big business now, but they are usually sold as such. It is as well to remember that it is an advantage for a shop to have an old piece, and it will usually be marked as such in justification of the price asked. Most dealers are knowledgeable and will give information about their wares. If no information can be given and questions evaded, then take another look and make sure you are getting value for money. A genuine old Toby will not be cheap, so it really depends on what you paid. There has certainly been no misrepresentation in this case, but I feel the jug has come in for a little treatment, in other words, faked to look older than it is. There is nothing wrong with reproduction if quality is maintained. Some 19th century reproductions are now antiques in their own right, and their value nearly as much as the pieces they were copied from.

Can you date a Rockingham cottage we have in our collection of china pieces? It is pure white and the raised flowers are painted in natural colours. It takes the form of a two-storey house with side buildings and a stepped approach. The base is hollow with a passage to the chimney. There are no marks on it to give a clue.

A Staffordshire porcelain pastille burner c. 1830

All pastille burners in the shape of cottages seem to be given the name of 'Rockingham' but so far no marked specimen has been recorded from that factory. Cottages were made in quite large numbers in the Stafford area in the 19th century and it is difficult to attribute them. This example is porcelain rather than pottery, and the flowers in high relief are in the style of some of the Rockingham encrusted pieces. Rockingham has become a traditional name which seems to be here to stay, but until some record is discovered, we shall never be sure if cottages were made there or not. This piece is about the nearest I have seen to the Rockingham style with characteristics which could point to that factory. These cottages were intended as fumiers and when placed over the aromatic cone, the perfumed smoke drifted up the chimney to percolate into the room. This one, unlike some, is really made to do the job and I would think it dates circa 1830.

It is not easy for the layman to distinguish pieces of china or know if a figure is choice or not. I am interested to gather a small collection of Dresden. Have you any helpful hints?

The products of the Meissen, (Dresden), factory are a very good choice for anyone to make, but unless you have almost unlimited funds you may need to content yourself with later 19th century work. The crossed swords mark in blue is the easiest to find. These have been faked so it is a case of judging quality and decoration.

The factory was established at Meissen early in the 18th century by Augustus, King of Poland. A chemist named Bottger began experimenting to find a true porcelain, long the secret of Chinese potters. He succeeded by using kaolin and the beautiful Meissen paste was developed. (There is a story that the white earth was discovered by a rider whose horse got bogged down in white mud, but we will leave that as I have heard a similar tale about Cooksworthy of Plymouth!) Fine modellers were used at Dresden, a notable name being that of Johann Kandler, who started at the factory about 1730; his work is highly prized. Early marks were in the form of A.R. monogram of Augustus Rex, but there are modern marks somewhat similar and can be seen on work from the Wolfson factory. There is a substantial difference in mark and decoration. If you find a crossed swords mark with a small nick across them, this indicates that the piece was sold 'in the white', and if the piece is decorated, this was done elsewhere. Two, three or four nicks means that the porcelain has faults, a small nick between the hilts or points indicates a very slight imperfection. Crossed swords with an 'S' is not a fake but a copy with no attempt to deceive. It will probably have been made by a Frenchman named Samson; he copied other notable factories with great skill. His work is collected in its own right.

Crossed swords with a star between the hilts denotes a definite

Above left and centre, *a pair of Dresden figures, Gallant and Maid.* Right, *a Dresden dessert tazza.* Below, *late 19th century Dresden monkey band figures*

period known as Marcolini, 1774 to 1814. Marks do help but must be coupled with good modelling and decoration, the hands on models are a good indication. Lacework on petticoats is particularly fine and looks real and no wonder, for actual lace was used. It was dipped in the clay and disintegrated during firing, leaving the natural effect. Figures are usually in pairs, such as Gallant and Maid in period dress. A tazza (a saucer-shaped container mounted on a pedestal foot and generally used for desserts) and a candelabra with a figure base are also worthwhile, and pieces with flowers in relief are a joy.

Pay a visit to a collection or museum to look at Dresden pieces. You can learn a great deal in this way which will stand you in good stead.

We have four figures which we know to be quite old, certainly 18th century. They are 9 inches tall and consist of the following: a girl holding a posy and wearing a pink coat, blue bodice, yellow skirt and bare feet; a boy with wheatsheaf and sickle, in white and gold shirt, green trousers and bare feet, with a straw beehive at his side; a boy wearing a black hat, blue coat, yellow breeches, with a hare in his satchel; a girl in a pale green dress, cerise skirt, holding a basket of fruit. All are on stump bases. There are no factory symbols but there are small discoloured patches on the bases. Can you suggest where they might have been made?

A set of 18th century Derby figures 'Four Seasons'

The Heath Brothers appear to have owned the Derby Pot Works up to the middle of the 18th century; it eventually failed and was sold up. At about this time a Mr Duesbury established himself in the pottery business, first as a salesman travelling about disposing of wares. William Duesbury had a hand in building a new factory in the 1750's for the manufacture of porcelain. Later he purchased the factory at Chelsea. Duesbury died in 1786 and a quite successful business came to his son, also named William. Derby figures of the first Duesbury period do not seem to have been marked, but it has been noticed that they have patch marks like you have mentioned, caused by standing on the saggar in the kiln. Strong stumps were necessary to prevent the figures warping during firing.

These figures are a set of the Four Seasons and are 18th century period as you suggest. They were probably made at the Derby factory of the first William Duesbury. To find this set free from damage and complete is a rare occurrence these days.

Can you tell us anything about an old Toby jug in our possession? It is the usual type figure with tricorn hat, brown coat, white breeches and stockings, black boots. He is seated and holding a frothing ale jug and mug and has a church warden clay pipe at his side. The glaze looks fairly thin. There is an impressed mark on the base, 'Ralph Wood, Burslem'. The figure is 9½ inches high.

A Ralph Wood Toby jug

The name Ralph Wood was in evidence right through the 18th century, for there were three of them from 1715 working as potters. You are fortunate to have a marked specimen; so many Toby jugs are unmarked. This piece seems to have the characteristic semi-translucent glaze, evident around the 1770's, the period of the son of the first Ralph Wood. The grandson of the first Ralph Wood followed into the business in the 1780's. Apart from Toby jugs, the Wood family made other figures and busts, as well as useful ware, and all are of considerable interest. There is a fine collection to be seen at the Victoria and Albert Museum in London, and it is as well for anyone contemplating the collection of Staffordshire Toby figures to take the opportunity to view the real thing.

There have been a vast number of reproductions through the years, and some downright attempts to fake. Colouring is an important factor. Early jugs had subtle hues because there were few colours available and these were not very strong. The glaze was translucent and, if crazed at all, is quite fine whereas attempts at imitation show craze marks much wider spaced and more pronounced. In later jugs, those of the 19th and 20th centuries, the colours are much too strong and definite.

The original Toby was used as a beer jug and is generally in the form of a stout, jovial man wearing cocked hat and breeches. Some favourite designs are: the English squire; John Bull; the Snuff Taker; the Sailor; Simple Simon; the Post Boy; the Watchman. There are also historical characters representing Nelson, Napoleon and others came later in varied colours. There are also later brown and salt glaze Toby jugs made by Doultons and others.

Early jugs are now difficult to find so, of necessity, the would-be collector must turn to the later 19th century examples. There are the better quality productions among these. No matter what you collect, let it be the finest examples you can find. Often the price difference between the good and the bad is not all that great.

I have always been attracted to painted enamel boxes and have gathered a small collection. Some have crack and chip damage, but this does not worry me too much as I have never paid a high price for any of them. They have been described as Battersea. One box measuring 2½ by 2 inches has the sides and base painted with flower sprays and on the lid, a battle scene with cavalry in the uniform of the Civil War period. There is a castle in the background. Another box about the same size is decorated with roses and a circular box has a shepherd boy, lamb, crescents and flowers. I also have three with mottos; 'Part not with me while we agree', 'A pledge of love', 'A token of regard' and on another, 'A trifle from Oxford'. Were these made at Battersea and how are they made?

Bilston enamel boxes

Enamel boxes make an attractive collection and although it is desirable to have undamaged examples, this is an area where there are a number of casualties. These boxes are frequently termed 'Battersea' but more often than not this is incorrect. Battersea was a centre of manufacture for a short time in the 18th century. Stephen Janssen started up in 1753 and made small items referred to as 'toys' at York House, a former residence of the Archbishops of York. Production was carried on for only three years and Battersea items are rare. The work was fine and can be distinguished as a result. Enamelling first required the skill of the metal worker who produced the base on which to work; this was then covered with a paste of powdered glass, which could be coloured if required by the addition of metalic oxides.

When placed in the kiln the enamel floats smoothly over the surface and adheres to the metal. The main area for enamel work in the 18th and 19th century was South Staffordshire, Bilston being the better-known name associated with the enamel work. Enamelled buttons were being made in the area during the first half of the 18th century. Furnaces used for enamelling were small and the size of the articles was limited. There was a great demand for snuff, patch and other boxes, also tea caddies, etui, pipe stoppers, nutmeg cases, scent bottles, brooches, buttons, spy glasses, condiment pots and a host of other small items, which offer a tremendous choice for the collector. A large number of enamellers worked in the Bilston, Wednesbury and Birmingham area, and it is impossible to attribute work to an individual. General terms 'Battersea' and 'Bilston' are used but the safest way is to say 'enamelled'. The boxes in question are from the South Staffordshire area rather than Battersea.

11 Treen

We have a rather unusual wooden object; it is made of mahogany and beautifully turned. It has the deep dull shine associated with wood that has been in use a long time. It seems to be some sort of grinder and we wonder what period it is. Can you help?

A Georgian coffee grinder

This is a coffee grinder of George III period and is placed in the collectors' category as 'Treen' (wooden bygones). These old grinders are quite rare these days. Coffee was first used as a beverage in Abyssinia before the 15th century. From there it spread to Arabia and Turkey at the beginning of the 15th century. In the 17th century coffee houses made their first appearance in Italy. The habit spread to Britain and the first coffee houses were opened in London in St. Michael's Alley, Cornhill, in 1652. Coffee drinking became popular, and the houses were places of social gathering and entertainment, remaining so well into the 18th century.

Your grinder will still do its job after all these years, and continue to have the patina which makes old wood so attractive.

Some years ago we inherited some pieces of furniture among which is a pair of oval buckets made from walnut wood. They are banded with five brass hoops and have brass handles. Each has a shaped brass liner. They are in perfect condition and we have resisted the temptation to use them as jardinieres. They measure 13 inches high and 14 inches across. Are they what are known as plate buckets?

These are not plate buckets but Dutch milk pails dating about 1790. They were used with a wooden yoke, which was shaped to fit the shoulders and had a chain and hook each side to hold the buckets. You may have seen them in Delft decorations. To find a pair of pails complete with their liners is quite rare. Although they might have made admirable plant holders, you have been wise to preserve them as ornaments. Once something is used for another purpose, there is a tendency to lose sight of the original attraction and quality. Good pieces should be preserved in original state and not adapted to other use. It would be nice if you could discover an old yoke to display with the buckets. It would make a conversation-piece collection and different, to say the least.

Among a collection of treen we have a turned mahogany vase, similar in shape to Sevres lidded vase with a square pedestal base. The cover has an acorn finial. The back of the vase is flattened and has a small hole drilled through. At the front there is a circular hole about 2 inches diameter and a block of wood behind this inside the vase. The piece is 9½ inches high. What was its original use?

A piece like this is quite rare in wood and more frequently seen in pottery or porcelain. It is a pocket watch holder which can either stand on a table or be hung on a wall, hence the flattened back. By removing the cover, the watch can be hung on the wood block which would normally have a small hook for the purpose.

This piece requires a watch, preferably early 19th century, and it would be worth while to spend a little time trying to find a silver timepiece which is, or can be put, in working order. Then not only will you have a display item, but a practical conversation piece.

We have what is thought to be an antique salt caster. It is made in walnut wood perfectly turned in two halves, which come together on a screw thread. There is a brass nozzle in the top through which salt is poured; we have tried it and it works perfectly. It looks quite old with the beautiful shine one sees on antique wood. There are four ball feet on the base made in brass. Are we right in thinking it is for salt?

You have tested your theory with modern free-running salt. Had you tried the more coarse block salt which was formerly used the result would have been different, for salt mined in previous centuries at Northwich, Droitwich and elsewhere was not the type to pour. Trenchers were used to hold salt for the table until a few years ago, with scoops to go with them.

You have an item which is quite rare and usually seen in box collections. It is time I told you that it is a Georgian string box. I do not know exactly when they arrived or who had the idea of putting the balls of string, which were sold by weight, into a very convenient dispenser. The box has taken on the patina we love to see as a result of age and waxing; it is a collector's piece and should be given a place of honour among the pieces you collect.

We have an unusual piece, the use for which has caused some speculation among our friends. The majority seem to think that it is a dessert trough. It is made in mahogany, which has the beautiful polish which one associates with age. It is shaped like a cradle, or rather a crescent moon quarter size. There is a division down the centre. The crescent overlaps the rectangular base which has brass cheese-shaped feet. Can you help?

This object is fairly rare these days. It is a period piece, cabinet-made for a special purpose and for use in the more salubrious household. You subconsciously arrived at the answer when you described the feet, for it is a Georgian cheese bucket. The shape supported a whole or half cheese and it was an essential piece of butler's furniture in those far off days before the pre-pack supermarkets, when a gentleman preferred to buy a whole cheese rather than a piece.

Unless you can resist the temptation to reveal the secret, here is another conversation piece. You could surprise your friends by placing a proper cheese in it at your next dinner party.

12   Copper, Brass, Pewter and Bronze

Can you give any information and possible date of a copper warming pan. It has a hinged lid which is chased with scroll patterns. The handle is plain turned and very smooth and looks old. The bottom of the pan shows burn marks. Were these placed in the fire to heat up?

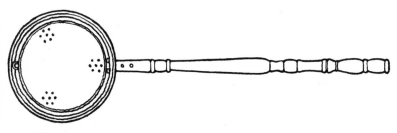

An 18th century warming pan

There seems always the desire to go to a warm bed. In olden times, a page found that one of his duties was to lie on his master's bed in order to warm it with his body!

Bed warmers first began to appear in the 16th century, made by both Dutch and English craftsmen. Some of the very early pans are dated, some also bear the armorials of the owners. It would indeed be rare to find one of these, and would be highly prized. The majority are 18th and 19th century; this one with a plain ash handle, of the former date but it is impossible to be more precise. The bed-warmer was not actually placed on the fire, but was loaded with hot embers or charcoal, then taken by a servant, and smoothed around in the bed to take off the chill. This method was quite efficient and continued until the copper and stone hot water bottles came into use.

The copper, (some were in brass), warming pan then became an item of decoration and still is an attractive piece to hang in the hall or beside the fireplace. Many reproductions have been made, so do look out for the older pans.

We have what we think is an 18th century copper coal scuttle. It is shaped like a helmet and in good condition. Are we correct with our date?

We must remember that coal receptacles have to take very heavy wear and tear. Coal was used as a fuel in the 18th century but a scuttle of the period would be hard to find. The surviving ones all seem to date 19th century. The helmet-shaped scuttles were exhibited at the Great Exhibition in 1851 and do not seem to have been made much earlier in any quantity. Even the bases of modern receptacles do not last very long and it is not unusual to find 19th century scuttles with a repair sheet riveted on.

Copies of the helmet shape are being made today in much thinner sheet copper and these frequently turn up in the smaller auctions. Even with the stressing, (simulated age), it is not difficult to realise that they are modern. Some even have china handles similar to the Victorian examples. I suppose some people might be fooled but the absence of the word 'antique' in the catalogue should give the intending buyer a clue. Your piece is obviously showing some age and is 19th century. Attractive copper scuttles find themselves used more as an ornament these days; they do brighten a room. I quite like them.

I have noticed that pewter prices are increasing of late, and I would be interested to know the probable age of a quart flagon with hinged lid. It is straight-sided, has a squarish 'C' handle and thumb piece. It was marked on the base but it is impossible to see what the marks were. It is rather black, should it be polished?

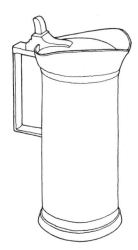

An 18th century pewter flagon

As you say, antique pewter has been on the up and up. It is certainly coming on the market less frequently. However, the opportunity still remains for those who are keen to make a collection. It is a case of waiting to pick up the desired piece at the right price. There is quite a fluctuation in prices, varying in different parts of the country. It is impossible to set a static value on any given piece. There was a revived interest in old English oak furniture, and pewter, (which goes very well with oak), seems to have followed it along.

Pewter is a very durable material and was introduced into Britain in Roman times. Interest faded out to be revived in the 14th century. For a long time it was mainly used in the church. The Pewters' Company was granted its first Charter in 1474 and its arms in 1479. It was quite a powerful body and had rights of Assay and search. Pewterers were required to register marks known as touch, much in the same way as goldsmiths and, from time to time, there were laid down standards.

The contents of pewter varied: the most common formula was 80 parts tin, 20 parts lead. 'Trifle' pewter; 79 parts tin, 15 parts antimony. 'Plate' pewter, 90 parts tin, 7 parts antimony, two bismuth, one part copper.

Touch marks enable makers to be traced and comprise of devices, initials or names, perhaps a combination of all. Flagons and mugs may bear house names of the inns where they were used. Earlier marks can be devices for the benefit of those who could not read, which would have applied to most of their customers in the 18th century. Early pewter is rare considering how much must have been made and there is a good reason for this. It was the practice to supply on a new for old system, consequently much went back into the melting pot. Most pewter available is 17th, 18th and 19th century. It is not confined to flagons and mugs; lots of useful ware, including salts, chargers, box and candlesticks, all make this collector's life interesting.

It is a pity that you could not define the mark which prevents attribution to a particular maker. Straight sided flagons were made earlier but the general style of yours dates it as 18th century.

With regard to polishing, this is a matter for individual decision, some collectors never clean and prefer to retain all the signs of accumulated age, others like the collection clean and shiny. I think you might strike a happy medium, clean but not thoroughly, leave some of the traces of age colour. A treatment with a mild abrasive polish once or twice a year should be sufficient to keep the flagon looking pleasant but not too new.

For many years we have used a rather unusual brass object as a door stop. It is cast in the form of a lion with only three legs, has a spout mouth and a hole in its back, with a lid. There has been some speculation as to its real use and the general opinion is that it was made as a lamp — the oil poured into the hole in the back and with a wick in the mouth. Have you any ideas?

This type of brass item is not a lamp but is known as an 'Aquamanile' and used as the name suggests, for holding water. They were modelled in various animal forms, equestrian knights, centaur and manlike figures. These vessels seemed to have arrived on the scene as early as the 12th century but I do not know of any very early pieces which have survived. Before the advent of knives and forks, food was eaten with the hands and required to be washed off the fingers between courses. The Aquamanile, filled with scented water, was brought with a bowl to the table for this purpose. They were made both in this country and on the continent; many came from the Dinnant area of Holland. Yours obviously has a cast line, therefore it is not one of the early pieces which were cast by the 'cire perdu' (lost wax) method. During the late 19th century there was a revived interest, not for use, but for ornament, and reproductions were made on a large scale. The tail of the animal usually curled over to form a handle. It would be difficult to find a genuine 15th century example outside a museum.

The use to which you put it is admirable and it has proved to be a conversation item.

Having bought a pair of 15 inch figures for £8 recently at an auction, we wonder why we were allowed to buy them so cheaply. They look like bronze, depict a farmer and his wife, and are mounted on black wood bases. They are not signed anywhere and the weight suggests that they are hollow. Could they be bronze?

One can still pick up a bargain at an auction sale, but I feel that you would not have got away with a pair of large bronzes at that price. Auctioneers generally know what they are selling and had these been bronze I think they would have bought them on the vendor's behalf. They do not usually allow valuable articles to go at ridiculously low prices. I am certain that your figures are made from a metal known as 'spelter', an alloy which is mainly constituted from zinc. It was much used in the second half of the 19th century to cast copies of master sculptors. Figures, animals and clock cases were made from it. It could be bronzed, lacquered, gilded or painted, or left in its natural lead like colour. Many clock cases were made and gilded to resemble the Louis style ormolu. There was considerable production on a mass scale, most seeming to have gone to Britain to help satisfy the insatiable demand made by the Victorians for ornament.

Spelter was cheap to produce and easy to work; it is fairly light in weight and often fixed to weighted bases. It has a ring if tapped, and is brittle in substance. There has not been much enthusiam for it so far, but I feel it is worthwhile to pick up a few pieces. Lesser items have suddenly come into popularity and in consequence values have risen substantially. This could well happen to spelter.

Are brass fenders of any particular value? I have one which is 56 inches long with pierced work all along the front; there are also thirty six brass flower heads dotted about. It has quite large brass paw feet. It would be interesting to know when fenders were first made.

Prior to the 18th century, wood was the staple fuel used in this country. Charcoal was the first coal used in industry and making it is an ancient art, its technique handed down from father to son. It was not just the case of building a pile of wood and covering it with clods; certain woods produced different results. For instance in the production of gunpowder, the best results came from willow, alder and dogwood. In domestic fireplaces wood was burnt on the floor of the hearth with andirons to support larger logs but when seacoal, as it was called in the 18th century, came into use, it had to be placed in a basket grate in order to allow the flow of air necessary for combustion. Fenders evolved with coal; at first a small piece of metal across the front of the basket. Heat discoloured the metal so it gradually got larger and further away, which encouraged more decorative shapes and pierced decoration. Some 18th century steel fenders of serpentine shape can still be found. In late 18th and early 19th century brass was used to a great extent and fenders became deeper and more ornate, with bars to support the sets of long handled fireirons then in use. Your fender is a Regency example and requires a set of irons and perhaps a pair of footmen to complete the picture and make a feature of the fireplace which, in spite of central heating, most people like to retain what was always considered the heart of the home.

One can hardly make a collection of fenders over and above the number of fireplaces available to display them, but one nice fender like your own is pleasant to live with.

Can you enlighten us about the signature on a small bronze, depicting two whippets, one running beside the other, on an oval base 9 inches long. It is signed Mene.

The bronze sculpture is the work of Pierre Jules Mene. He was born in Paris 1818 and died in 1879. His interest in bronze no doubt came from his father who was a worker in metals. Mene, although no doubt influenced by the great Masters, had a beautiful style all his own and was very successful in his lifetime. He was part of the French School known as 'animaliers' in the 19th century. In company with Barye and others who enjoyed the love of animal sculpture, he left for us a range of fine pieces to be collected. Mene exhibited at the Paris Exhibition and received many awards for merit. So much was Mene thought of in France, he was awarded the title 'Chevalier de la Legion d'Honour' for his service to Art.

Work by this sculptor has come into prominence among collectors in the last few years and values have risen steadily, but there are still examples to be discovered. The work is beautiful and well worthwhile. Probably one of his best known works is 'The Accolade', the two horses forming a quite powerful bronze. Work by Mene can still be found in auction catalogues and there are shops specialising in Animalier bronzes for the discerning collector. There is no doubt that there are still pieces in possession of those who are not aware of the value.

Having acquired two horse brasses, would it be worth adding to them and making a collection?

Horse brasses have always been a form of decoration; they have been used for hundreds of years in some form or another. Genuine old brasses are not easy to find but worth looking for. The market has been saturated with modern reproductions. These are quite attractive in their way, but not for the collector. Very few dray and cart horses remain in regular use; some of the brewery companies still retain teams and they can often be seen at shows and in street processions bedecked in beautiful shining brass. There must still be some old brasses lying around in country stables, but most have found a home in which to hang. There are a host of designs, some showing the owner's trade, windmills for millers, milk churns for dairies, anchor sign of St Nicholas, patron Saint of sailors, for barge and dock horses, barrels for breweries, and so on. Trade signs make good specialist collections. There are many brasses involving superstition, hearts for longevity, crescents to ward off evil, etc.

When considering a brass, examine it for workmanship, wear, and signs of age. Reject the pieces which are rough and obviously cast. Horse brasses require to be displayed en masse, and if you can, find some still on leather. A martingale is attractive, also the rare 'flyer' which was fastened above the animal's head with a small brass or a bell swinging in a frame. I do not consider a collection complete without a pair of hames, (horn-like pieces) which were worn on each side of the collar.

Do make a collection, but be selective and choose only the best examples.

Would it be possible to near date a copper coach horn, which was discovered in the cellar of an inn, still in a dilapidated leather case? The horn is 46 inches long.

These horns are rightly named, carried as they were on coaches. Stage coaches were the forerunners of the now vast public transport system. From 1874 they also carried official mail, the first mail coach running between London and Bristol. 18th century coaches were fairly heavy vehicles and travelled slowly, but in the 19th century they were built much lighter and could reach up to twelve miles per hour. Mail coaches kept a strict schedule, the time allowed from London to York was twenty hours. Teams of horses required quick changes at the recognised stations; the sound of the horn heralded their approach and warned the hostlers to be ready.

Your horn would, I think, date circa 1840 and if you can possibly renovate the case, it should be kept with it as a collector's piece. Leather or wicker cases were strapped to the coach and kept the horn protected and handy. Older horns had plate or silver mouth-pieces, the latter generally hallmarked and therefore can be accurately dated. Genuine horns are tuned and quite easy to distinguish from the vast number of reproductions which have been made, rough brazing and mouth pieces always give these away.

Three circular brass wall plaques have been given to me. They are about 12 inches diameter and show sailing ships and a biblical scene in raised pattern. The brass is very thin and they appear to have been lacquered. Are they old?

Some of these pieces can be old but in this case they are modern. The specimens are hammered brass ware, usually called dinanderie, much of which was manufactured in the district around Dinant, Belgium. Modern work is not of very good quality, being produced in commercial quantity for the mass market.

The older pieces were heavier and better decorated in the manner of old woodcuts. Older items, particularly tobacco boxes in Dutch style, coffer boxes, and plaques, are worth collecting; they can be distinguished by comparing quality and workmanship. Modern plaques, coal boxes, etc., are quite decorative. Most are lacquered from necessity, for constant cleaning would soon cause holes to appear in the thin gauge metal.

Our bronze figure of a crouched panther has always been much admired. It is 7 inches long and is boldly signed Barye on the rock type base. Recently learning that this sculptor is quite famous, I am wondering if this small item has any great value?

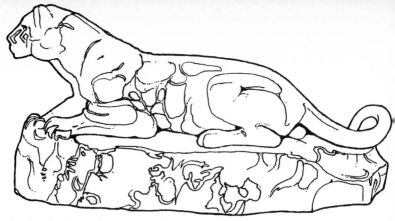

An Antoine Barye bronze panther

Antoine Louis Barye was born in Paris 1796. He is considered the father of all French 19th century animaliers. Trained as a goldsmith, even in his early years he became very interested in modelling small animals. The interest gained momemtum and he was prompted to take every opportunity for the study of animals, visiting zoos and fairs. He even dissected a carcass if it came his way, in order to further his knowledge of animal anatomy. During his early years as a goldsmith, Barye studied design with Gros and Basio. When he was 23 years old, he received a Salon award for a lithograph. By 1831 he had exhibited several bronze works in Paris, mainly busts for which he also obtained awards. The Salon was not very interested in his animal pieces and this attitude upset him. It was no doubt this disapproval by the Salon committee that spurred him on to further animal creations, which were certainly approved by the public. He also received government orders when animal works were commissioned. Barye, unlike other sculptors, set up his own foundry and often cast his own creations. Clockcases, candle sticks, and other ornamental pieces were also designed and made.

For his work, Louis was created an Officer of the Legion of Honour. When he was 62 years old, he was elected a Member of The Academy of Fine Arts. He was a great influence on other French sculptors of the 19th century, including Rodin.

Earlier works by Barye are considered the more desirable being cast by the 'lost wax' method. Later the sand casting process was used. The panther specimen certainly has a fair value, and works by this artist, (who died in 1875), are considered very collectable.

13 Pictures and Prints

Are Baxter prints worth collecting and what are the special points to look for? How were these prints first made?

'The Bridesmaid' a print by George Baxter

There does not seem to be a great mass of collectors for Baxter prints, but they do have their devotees and, after having been neglected for many years, they are exciting interest. However, there is still time to make a collection at a reasonable cost.

George Baxter, born in 1804, started his working life as a printer. Later he became an illustrator and wood block engraver among other things, for he was quite diverse in occupations. Baxter's father, John, was also a printer and together they published the Baxter Illustrated Bible and Album which necessitated the cutting of a very large number of wood blocks for its pictures.

He always had a great ambition to produce prints in many colours, which would look like paintings. After much work and experiment, it is safe to say, he was successful in his efforts. After he had devised a master steel plate, he obtained a patent for his process, colour printing in oils, about 1836. It was a slow and lengthy process. Apart from the master plate, a number of wood blocks had to be cut to produce the separate colours and shading, some pictures involving twenty or more blocks. Printing was done on a hand press and everything had to be in perfect register. Previous to his using oil, Baxter experimented with water colour and produced a fine print called 'Butterflies'. This spurred him on. Eventually, he realised his ambition to produce a print which really did resemble a painting and decided that his work should be for the enjoyment of the masses. Some prints were sold for as little as one and sixpence.

Baxter's early prints depicted moral subjects, for he was a religious man. Later subjects were more romantic.

Baxter's prints of Queen Victoria's coronation and other state occasions, together with quite good portraits of the Queen, brought him some recognition. At the Great Exhibition in Hyde Park in 1851, he took a stall and displayed a collection of his work. In spite of all his work and quite large sales, Baxter never seemed to prosper and was always in some financial difficulty.

Baxter sold licences for the use of his process to others, the most notable buyer being Abraham Le Blond. Finally, George Baxter retired from business and went to live in Kent, where he died in 1867.

The would-be collector has a range of some four hundred good subjects to choose from. There are also series prints well worth attention, and the ones commemorating the 1851 Exhibition show the great Crystal Palace.

As with many things, there are imitations and fakes. Genuine prints bear the signature imprinted on the picture itself. After 1848, a red oval seal was used on the border with name, address and title. After 1850 a white seal was embossed on the border with name and address.

Always look for unfaded prints with complete mounts. Some prints are rare, others quite plentiful but if you like what you see, then collect it.

The picture illustrated gives some idea how fine the prints can look. It shows a Victorian miss, known as 'The Bridesmaid'. This one is not particularly rare and often comes up at auction.

A guide to dating can be obtained from the different addresses on the mounts. Kings Square circa 1830; Northampton Square 1843 to 1860. Early prints were enclosed in a blue ruled border.

By the way, imitation prints seldom have fast colours and will run if damped. Baxter's should never be hung in direct sunlight.

As we have some pictures by Alfred Montague, we would like to know the period in which he was working. It is presumed he was English. Are pictures by him worth anything?

Yes, pictures by this artist are fairly valuable. He worked from London 1832 until 1883. A known painter of landscapes and marines, he travelled quite a lot on the continent painting town and coastal scenes. He also travelled round the coasts of the British Isles. Alfred Montague became a Member of the Society of British Artists and had work accepted for exhibition at the Royal Academy. He also exhibited at the Suffolk Street Galleries and at the British Institute. He was quite fond of painting off-shore scenes and fishing boats, battling with

A pair of seascapes by Alfred Montague

heavy seas was a favourite subject, the cloud and sea effects reflecting the mood.

Sea pieces are worth well into three figures, so your collection has value as well as some joy to you.

Alfred Montague exhibited over one hundred and fifty works, so you should still be able to discover others. I believe you can see a 'Shipwreck' piece by him at the Salford Museum.

Living·in Yorkshire and blessed with an old house which has open fireplaces and lots of oak beams, we find that sporting prints and pictures go well in this atmosphere. We have an·oil painting on canvas of a hunting scene signed Dalby York, but cannot discover anything about this artist. Can you help?

'A Hunting Scene' by David Dalby

York is not a surname but the city. David Dalby came from this part of the world, living in Leeds and York up to about the middle of the 19th century. The late 18th and early 19th centuries produced a crop of sporting painters and Dalby was among them. He is not as well known as some of his contemporaries, mainly because he did not bother to exhibit at any of the fashionable venues. He gained a good living by private commissions and painted racehorses for owners, also hunting scenes, (in which the characters could be recognised), other sporting scenes and mail coaches. He also painted portraits of prominent locals.

There was also a John Dalby in the same area, painting much in the style of David. Both produced quite good quality work and are equally well thought of.

It might well be that David added York to his signature in order to distinguish his work from that of John, who was last recorded in 1853. As you live in the area a little research at Leeds or York may unearth some local data. Librarians, I find, are quite helpful and willing to delve into the archives.

You might possibly discover other works by this artist in your area and add to your collection. The short cropped tails of the horses, incidentally, are an interesting characteristic of the period.

George and Oliver Clare seem to be comparatively well known, but we do not seem to be able to find any reference to Vincent Clare. The picture is a small one showing a robin's nest in a broken apple blossom bough, resting on a leafy mossy bank. Can you enlighten us?

As you say, George and Oliver Clare are known. Vincent painted very much in the same manner and that is not surprising for they were

'Still Life' by Vincent Clare

related. Vincent was born in 1855 and died in 1925. He, like his kinsfolk, worked quite a lot in the Birmingham area. It would be worth visiting the art auctions there if you are looking for more works by Vincent Clare. His signature is not easy to spot, usually very neatly tucked away in the composition near the bottom right of the picture. Vincent is known as a still life artist. His work is true to nature and one cannot help but admire his small pictures.

George and Oliver Clare both exhibited in London at the Royal Academy and Suffolk Street Galleries. Vincent does not appear to have bothered with the fashionable venues.

All the Clares appear to have been influenced by W.H. Hunt, (William Henry, not William Holman), who became known as 'Birds-nest Hunt'. His pictures of nature are well worth collecting if you like hedgerow landscapes.

Vincent Clare's work can be acquired at very reasonable price; it is not generally considered as good as the others, but 'beauty is in the eye of the beholder!' It is sufficient that a picture pleases one's personal taste.

We have a mezzotint picture; can this process be explained?

A mezzotint is a print which has usually been taken from a copper plate engraving. It is by far the best process for reproducing copies of Master works, particularly portraiture. Invented on the continent by Ludwig von Seigen, the process was introduced in to Britain in the 1660's. There have been many fine mezzotint engravers. Early names like William Sherwin and Isaac Bennett are not easy to find. Later names like William Penther, John Smith and James MacArdell, who worked in the 18th century, and 19th century engravers such as

Charles Turner and S.W. Reynolds, are among those whose work is worth looking for. As in other similar processes, a properly prepared and polished copper plate of even thickness is first prepared. The preliminary task for the engraver is time-consuming and involves the use of a rocking tool, which looks something like a bolster chisel with rounded blade. The edge is very finely serrated and is rocked over the plate in all directions, but to a planned system, in order to reach the desired effect which consists of close dot indentations to form a burr. The subject is then etched in with a steel engraving point. Next, the metal is scraped away at various depths in order to form the light and dark shade areas.

When the engraving is complete, a proof print is made so that any imperfections can be spotted. The plate is heated and treated with an ink mixture, comprising charcoal and burnt linseed oil in a thick consistency. After this has been applied to the plate with a special brush, the surplus is wiped off and a proof is made under pressure in the press. Several proofs may be required before all the imperfections are corrected and the engraver is satisfied. Before the process of facing copper plates with steel by electrical deposit evolved in 1880, engraved plates soon became worn and only a limited number of good prints could be made. Early plates are therefore the best examples, and should be the aim of serious collectors. Worn plates do not show the same completeness, fineness and clarity of line.

I have seen mezzotints kept in folders; this is a mistake and can harm the print face. They should always be in bordered frames to ensure good preservation. One of the greatest exponents of mezzotint engraving, whose work is still available in reasonable quantity, was Francesco Bartolozzi, (1725-1815). He left Italy about 1764, went to England, and left again in 1813 to work in Lisbon, where he died.

Mezzotint engravings can make a most interesting and worthwhile collection on permanent view in your home and are not outrageously expensive.

Is the artist A. Pollentine a very well known Italian painter? His pictures of the Venetian scene are very colourful. We have a work by him but do not know anything of the artist's history.

It can be understood why you have thought A. Pollentine an Italian artist. The 'A' stands not for an Italian christian name, but the quite English Alfred. Actually he came from London, but painted for a great deal of his time in Venice.

The Grand Canal features quite a lot in his compositions. He always liked to include foreground figures either in boats or on the terrace walks. His architectural background is precise and the pictures have depth.

The Grand Canal, Venice by Alfred Pollentine

Pollentine exhibited at the British Institute, Suffolk Street Galleries, and of course, in his beloved Venice from the years 1861 until 1880. I feel he has been neglected in the past, but is now becoming well thought of among collectors. There is still time to acquire work by this artist at a reasonable price, at least for his smaller works. Larger canvasses are getting into the four figure bracket, when they come to auction. The work of this painter can promote a panoramic decorative effect and should be properly lit and given a reasonable amount of wall space, where they can be enjoyed to the full.

Are paintings on glass collectors' items? Is it best to look for those signed by the artist?

Glass pictures were made as early as the 17th century but these are very rare. Those worked in the 18th and early 19th century are easier to come by. If you are deciding to collect, it is just as well to know a little about the subject. They are not original paintings as we generally understand it. They start out as a print. The process commences with a sheet of glass and a mezzotint print. The print is firmly and evenly cemented to the glass. When dry, the paper is removed; this is achieved by damping and gently removing the resultant pulp. The outline of the print adheres to the glass and requires several coats of transparent varnish. When this is dry, the colours of the original are painted in separately to create the picture. Actually no paint touches the glass at all. The result is quite fascinating and you will find them attractive.

A collector must have an eye to quality; I have seen some rather bad examples, mainly 19th century. Some subjects are better than others, so look for portraits after the great painters and prints after such artists as Watteau. These are quite good. Sometimes the signatures of engravers can be found transferred from the print. Examples from the late 18th century are in my opinion the best, especially if in their original frames.

There are modern fakes about, so it is well to bear in mind that old glass which was fairly thin had a number of imperfections. Modern glass cannot be made to imitate these. Once you have seen a few good 18th century examples it will not be difficult to spot the imitations.

We have a small water colour drawing of a cottage interior. The family are poorly dressed and it shows two of the children in the foreground looking at a bird in a cage. The drawing has great charm and measures only 6½ inches by 9½ inches. The signature looks to be Tom Faed. Is the artist known?

The artist is reasonably well known, especially for domestic genre scenes like this one. The children are probably admiring a linnet. In the 19th century it was the practice to trap and cage these wild birds as songsters.

Thomas Faed was born at Kirkcudbright, Scotland, in 1826. He moved to London in 1852, where he was quite popular and exhibited a large number of works at the Royal Academy. He was elected a Royal Academician in 1864. He liked to paint Scottish peasant life and you are in possession of an example of a croft interior. Faed died in London in 1900.

I have seen pictures painted in a rather unusual and interesting style. They are very amusing. The signature is 'Romyn'. They are probably 19th century. Do you have any information about this artist?

The pictures you have seen are the work of Conrad Romyn, born in 1915. He is a dedicated painter who has made an impression on contemporary art. His work is poetic and humanistic, and, having a great love for the theatre and circus, he chose some most interesting subjects. Romyn studied in Amsterdam before the second world war, then, like most of his age, got caught up in the holocaust and served in several areas including the Far East. After the war he continued his studies in Paris and Rome and became a professional artist. His figures and landscapes have a style all their own, aping none, but he does like to mix his paints in the manner of the Old Masters. His work has been displayed in several exhibitions, including the Royal Academy, O'Hara Gallery, London, Stockholm and Paris: His work

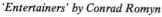
'Entertainers' by Conrad Romyn   *'Virtuoso' by Conrad Romyn*

hangs in several private collections and in the National Museum, Stockholm. Romyn is still painting at his studio in Surrey.

I, too, find Romyn's work interesting; the expressions he captures in some of his clownish pictures cannot help but attract attention and admiration.

We have a picture on canvas said to be by William Shayer. It measures 16 inches by 21 inches inside the frame. About what period is the picture, and is the painter of any particular importance?

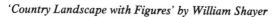
'Country Landscape with Figures' by William Shayer

Is it Antique?

Often people have pictures which they have lived with for a long time and which have quite a value, but they have never bothered to find out about them. In consequence, they are not insured against loss and sometimes owners can be persuaded to part with them at far below the current value. Work by William Shayer is reasonably valuable, some of it in excess of £1,000.

William Shayer was quite talented. He was a native of Southampton who found he had a natural gift and took advantage of it. I do not think he ever took any lessons.

Born in 1788, he lived a long life, missing his centenary by one year. Living as he did on the edge of the New Forest, landscape subjects were on his doorstep as it were and he became very fond of working in the area. He included much of the gypsy life which abounded in the Forest in those days. Eventually the forest scene was exhausted and Shayer turned to coastal scenes which included fisher folk, much as he had included the gypsies.

Over his long life he painted a great number of pictures. He was a Member of the Society of British Artists and exhibited a large number of works in London, at the Suffolk Street Galleries and some at the Royal Academy from 1820 onwards.

This artist has work at the Victorian and Albert Museum and in some provincial museums. He is reasonably important and his forest and coastal scenes are worth collecting.

Having a picture which is something like the rustic scenes painted by George Morland, we were wondering if you can recognise the artist, for on the doorpost there is some writing which looks like a signature beginning with the letter H. It is on canvas which has been relined, size about 16 inches by 19 inches. Can you offer any suggestions?

'Country Landscape with Animals and Figures' by John Herring

The work could well be that of John Frederick Herring who was born in the county of Surrey in 1795. From humble beginnings as a stable hand he progressed to gain experience in the Arts by learning sign writing. Like others of his day, he found a patron interested enough to finance proper tuition and he went to study with Abraham Cooper.

In the early 19th century, sporting pictures were in fashion and Herring moved into this field. He obtained commissions to paint racehorses and did quite well. He became known as a sporting painter, but his roots in the country still prompted him to paint animals and birds. As the years passed he spent more time with farmyard scenes. Herring was a prolific painter and exhibited at the Royal Academy and elsewhere in London from 1818.

His work sold quite well in his lifetime, and has continued to do so up to the present day, particularly racehorse subjects. He died in Tunbridge Wells in 1865. It is as well to note that his son John Frederick was also an artist, painting much in his father's style and also copied some of his father's work. He exhibited in London, mostly at Suffok Street galleries, also at the Royal Academy. It is small wonder that on occasions his work is mistaken for that of his father. Herring Junior died 1907. Both are worth collecting — Herring senior's work is generally the more expensive.

I have rather a nice water colour drawing of wild birds in natural habitat. It is signed A. Thorburn. Do you have any information about this artist?

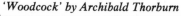

'Woodcock' by Archibald Thorburn

Above, 'The Covey at Daybreak'. Below, 'Pheasants'. Both by Archibald Thorburn

Archibald Thorburn was born near Edinburgh in 1860. He studied with his father, a talented painter of miniatures. Archibald was primarily a naturalist and painted birds, mammals and flowers; it is for his bird drawings that he is best known. He was a book illustrator and also wrote books on wild life. His work was much admired during his lifetime and he exhibited at the Royal Academy. The last years of his life were spent in Surrey where he died in 1935. He was a great friend of John Lodge, also a naturalist painter. John Southern, a friend of mine, who admires these two artists, has set up a permanent Memorial Exhibition at 'Penmount', Liskeard, in Cornwall. This is a unique collection acquired by him over many years, and well worth a visit when you are in the West Country.

Among a lot bought at auction was a coloured wax plaque about eight by four inches. It is in relief and shows workers in the field in attitude of prayer. It has the title 'Angelus'. There is an initial 'A.O.' on the edge. It looks old; can you say what it is?

Ivorex plaques. Left, *Lady Godiva.* Right, *St Paul's Cathedral.* Below, *Shakespeare's house*

Country crafts are always an interesting research. These items were made by Arthur Osborne who worked at Faversham in Kent. Production started 1899 as a cottage industry. Osborne first carved the subjects, then transferred the image to a gelatine mould. Refined Newark plaster was poured in and, when set, it was painted in water colours. After the paint had dried the subject was passed through a hot wax bath, then finally polished. Some four hundred different subjects were used, including historic buildings, and scenes from Scott, Pickwick, Burns and Shakespeare.

From small beginnings the business expanded and orders were dispatched by the crate all over the British Isles, the United States, India and Australasia. Mechanical production to cope with the great demand was tried but failed; the process demanded hand work and some twenty people were employed in the production. Arthur Osborne died in 1943. His work remains to puzzle most people. The plaques are not very valuable at the moment, but a collection of 'Ivorex', (the name given to them), might become more valuable in the future.

14 Miscellaneous

While on holiday we spent a day at an auction and thoroughly enjoyed it. To buy was a temptation which could not be resisted and we came away the owners of a Persian rug. It is in perfect condition and measures four feet three and a half inches one way by six foot eleven inches the other. The pattern has flowers and sprays all over on a whitish and red background. Would you think it is antique? As we are now interested in purchasing more Oriental rugs, can you offer any advice?

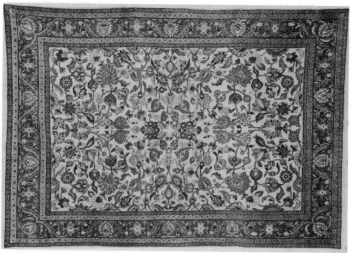

A Persian rug

As you say, a day at auction is quite enjoyable. If the rug had been an antique the auctioneers would have catalogued it as such. You have no doubt bought a fairly modern rug.

Oriental rugs are still made in quantity, but few in the truly Nomad method. This rug is in the pattern of Kashan (which is in central Persia) an area which has a number of rug centres, providing patterns like Isfahan, Senneh, Saruk and Ferrahan, to name a few of the more popularly known.

Modern rugs are plentiful and quite a number are imported each year. It is the older rugs which are sought by collectors. Some rugs have quite bright colours, but there are good specimens which are not so colourful. Often when rugs from private sources come to auction, they are fairly dirty. The changes can be amazing when they have been cleaned by a specialist. I emphasise the word 'specialist', for a rug in the hands of an inexperienced person could prove a disastrous!

There are several points which can be of help. It would be wise to read a little about the subject. There are informative reference works obtainable, which will give you the theory which must then be backed up by practical experience. Visit museums and private collections whenever possible, in order to learn to recognise a good rug. A reputable dealer will generally help and advise you to buy from his stock. His good name depends on giving his customers value for money and many dealers are most knowledgeable about the trade. Most people buy their first rug at auction, where there will be competition from the Trade for first class items. They know what they are buying and people follow their lead.

Always examine a rug. Look for evidence of worn pile which has been touched in to disguise it. The back will often reveal more than the front. Look for a close knot. Repairs can be seen, but do not reject on this account, if they have been well executed, bearing in mind that expert renovation is not cheap and money would not generally be spent on a poor rug.

Care of a rug is important — brush or light vacuum. If the latter, any beater action should be disconnected; many fringes have been destroyed by use of these. Rugs do get dirty, so need an occasional specialist clean. Rugs with tears can be repaired by the experts. Roll rather than fold for storage. Long periods of folding can split or weaken the rug.

Quite often you may see a rug which appears to be faded in one part all the way across. The reason for this is that they were made by families often on the move. Wool was collected from the sheep or goats, spun, and then dyed in different areas. The changes in vegetation as the family moved and the rug progressed affected the colour. It is this which gives the faded impression.

Nomads wove on a simple frame, often four branches bound together, the size depending on the intended rug. The warp threads stretched across to form the basis for the weaver, or weavers, for they often worked together. Pieces of wool about two inches long formed the loop (or knots, as we term them) deftly used in different colours to form the pattern. Children were trained in the art from a very early age and their nimble fingers made the finest rugs.

After completion, the rugs look quite rough and have to be carefully shorn to produce a fine pile.

If you consider that a fine wool rug can have three to four hundred knots to the square inch, and a silk one seven to eight hundred, the value can be appreciated. The closeness of the knot is the guide to quality. When you turn a good rug over, the pattern will be seen to be as good at the back as at the front. Depth of pile varies with the areas in which the rug was made. In hot areas, a short pile; in cold areas, a longer pile. Not all rugs are actually made in Persia, hence the term Oriental is applied generally. It is common to hear a Bokhara or Tekke rug termed Persian.

Look for rugs which are complete with borders and original fringes; these are made from the loose ends of the warp. Feel a rug, old ones are fairly limp. I have often heard the saying, 'The softer the feel, the richer the Persian!' I think this is a good guide, the best rugs being silk followed by under neck wool, which is very soft. The making of many imported modern Oriental rugs in mechanised. If in doubt, look at the fringe; these are always applied. These rugs are also much stiffer.

The Persian rug and carpet arrangement is quite different to that of European rugs. A tent or room in Persia is laid out with a large rug in the centre, and four longer, narrower rugs (which we would term runners) round the sides. It is worth remembering that the finest rugs were made to look at, not to be walked on. You often see them draped in old paintings.

Care should be taken in placing rugs — avoid areas of heavy tread or in front of open fireplaces where sparks can cause damage. (There are coarser and cheaper Oriental rugs which look quite nice and can be used in these areas.)

The range of Oriental rugs is enormous, but with experience, you will learn to identify many of them. Treated properly, a good rug will last for generations; so invest in the best you can afford, for your own pleasure and later for your family.

There seems to be quite an interest in doll collecting now. Having two dolls which are rather nice, and retained from my childhood days, I would like to start a collection. Have I left it too late?

A late 19th century German doll

It is never too late to start a collection, no matter the subject. Considering that every little girl was surrounded with dolls for years past, it is impossible to say how many are available to the collector. They are still being made in most countries of the world, so the supply is continuous. Most collectors would wish to concentrate on the productions of the 19th century and naturally some dolls are quite rare. Dolls have existed since goodness knows when, examples have been unearthed from ancient Egyptian and Roman times, also from other early civilisations. Whether they were playthings or idols must be left to the imagination. There is the thought that doll may have evolved from idol. These early pieces show evidence that they were made with movable limbs.

Unless you are going to buy every doll you see, some time must be spent in making a study of the subject, reference works are available. One of the problems is display, so speciality is the order of the day. There is not much fun in having a large number of dolls tucked away in trunks. For instance, you may choose 19th century Pedlar dolls; these are what the name suggests. The interest is as much in the ware they have about their person and in the tray and baskets held, as in the doll itself, which can often be quite crude, with kid, papier mache, wood or perhaps wax faces. The dolls are usually dressed in either male or female country style and indeed, follow the style of the individuals who actually peddled wares from door to door.

The genuine Pedlar dolls were a cottage craft, often made as an amusing occupation or sold for pin money. Some of the actual makers are known. Genuine early 19th century examples are quite rare. If a doll looks rather too nice, it usually means a later made-up job. Examine the wares, they should be in keeping with the period.

Wax dolls, which can date quite early, could be a theme for a specialist range, as could mechanical dolls with walking and other movement mechanisms.

There remains the French and German bisque and porcelain productions. Many have marks of identification and can be traced to such makers as Simon and Halbig, Rohmer and Simonne, together with a number of others. The doll illustrated is a German bisque head of the late 19th century. There are also English-made dolls to consider. Those with names such as Goss are worth looking for. The range is wide and there are specialist dealers. The history of dolls exists to be read. The way is clear for anyone who wants to start a collection.

Some time ago when we moved into an old house we had bought, there was a lead plate on the wall which we understand was a Firemark. One day a gentleman knocked on the door and offered to buy it. We agreed a price, and he removed it. Do you think we did right to part with it?

A lead firemark

Providing you obtained a price which satisfied you at the time there can be no regrets. The plate might well have disappeared in the night at some time or another anyway. Firemarks are collectors' pieces these days and rare ones are commanding good prices. It is advisable to bring old plates in out of the cold. The Great Fire of London seems to have started the Fire Insurance business and it began to get established about 1680. In order to protect their own interests, Insurance Companies formed their own separate firefighting services. At first they refused to co-operate with each other but there were amalgamations in London about 1825, and in 1833 ten offices joined to form the London Fire Engine Establishment, later to become a public body and ultimately the Fire Brigade as it is known today. Firemarks were attached to buildings to indicate which Company held the risk. The early marks, made in lead, displayed the policy number. Marks were designed in such a way that they were instantly recognised by illiterate firemen, who would only fight a fire in a building holding their own Company's policy. If it was not their Company it was too bad — and away they went!

Old lead marks with numbers are the more valuable. After about 1800 copper, iron, and tin were used. The Insurance Companies also formed services in provincial towns, so marks can be found all over the country. There are genuine modern plates issued by some Companies which will no doubt become collectors' items in the future. There are also reproductions of old plates being made for sale. They should be sold as such, but human nature being what it is, some may be misrepresented. There is a need to examine and ask for authentication when paying a good price.

Would an old gas cycle lamp be worth keeping? It is in good condition with reflector and glass intact.

Yes, I think it would. Acetylene gas was used for car and cycle lamps and also for home lighting. The gas is produced by water action on calcium carbide, forming hydrocarbon gas (C_2H_2). One pound of carbide produces about five cubic feet of gas and yields a spectrum very similar to daylight. It is a very hot burner and, with temperatures over 3,500 degrees centigrade, is also used for cutting and welding hard metals.

Your lamp will have two compartments, one for water at the top, allowing a drip feed, which is cut off by gas pressure. The flame works on the bunsen principle of getting as much air as possible to the gas as it leaves the burner.

The cases of cycle lamps were usually plated on brass; copper cannot be used as it is affected chemically by this gas. When properly adjusted the carbide lamps give off a bright white light and were in popular use late 19th and early 20th century. Although not yet antique, not many seem to have survived in good condition; most were discarded, causing some rarity. In good condition, your lamp should be preserved; it is a decorative conversation piece, and no doubt will become an antique for future collectors.

Among our cabinet collection of small pieces of a general nature are one or two small carved ivory items which we know to be Netsuke. We would like to know something about them. Are they of any special value?

Examples of Japanese Netsuke in ivory

The Netsuke, or end piece, was part of a personal accessory in Japan and elsewhere in the Orient where a sash was worn. The Japanese traditional clothing was devoid of pockets and the only place to carry small personal possessions was in the sash, called an 'obi'. The possessions were tied with cord to the end of a piece of bamboo stick and tucked into the obi. About the year 1700, the odd carved decoration appeared on the ends of the sticks and it was not long before the carving became more elaborate and the art of Netsuke carving was under way. By the 18th century all sorts of materials were used as end pieces — wood of different hues, mammal and marine ivory, quartz, and lacquer work among them. The Netsuke became a status symbol and became a subject for presentation.

There is no limit to the different subjects represented in the carvings, birds, animals, reptiles, insects, flowers, shell fish, mythical and religious symbols and the more numerous 'Katabori' figure carvings. There were many specialist carvers whose work is highly prized among collectors today.

It is always nice to see a Netsuke attached by a cord to an Inro, the name given to the compartmented box used to carry items like medicines and seals. The cord passes round the box and through a small bead, often also carved. The box is closed by sliding the bead down, reversing the process to open it. Some Netsukes can be quite expensive and to make a serious collection in this field, a study is necessary. Age is not always the criterion, for the 19th century produced many fine artists of high standing whose work is prized by serious collectors. Many Netsukes are signed but this does not necessarily prove the piece. The work and signatures have been copied and it needs an expert to identify these, for they are made by practised carvers. The price to pay is the main concern. There are fakes and the worst possible example I have seen were of a reconstituted material which looked like ivory. They were catalogued Netsuke, but there was no mention of ivory. I tried to warn the intending buyer, but was accused of wanting the lot myself. It gave me no particular satisfaction to see them bought at a ridiculously high price.

Few can resist the attraction of the Netsuke, there is some merit in all the genuine carved examples. Little groups like the boy being released from the trap set by the 'Tengu' Goblin of the forest, who waylays the stray to instil him with evil thoughts, or the monkey trainer, and other small figures, all of which are pleasing to the eye.

Any cabinet collection of small pieces can be enhanced by the addition of a few of these delightful ornamental items.

The advent of western dress has not prevented the continuation of the art, which has extended through to the present century. Contemporary artists are as skilful as ever.

I have recently become interested in Antiques, and would like to visit an auction sale. I have heard people talk about conditions of sale and buyers' rings so I am a bit put off. Can you explain about these things?

Conditions of Sale are laid down by the auctioneers. In the main they are fairly general and most contain the following clauses: the highest bidder to be the buyer, and no bidding shall be retracted. If any dispute arises, the Auctioneer shall have absolute discretion to settle it, and if he thinks fit, offer the disputed lot again. The bidding shall be at the discretion of the Auctioneer, who may refuse a bidding and withdraw any lot from sale. No transfer of any lot will be permitted or recognised.

All lots are put up for sale subject to any reserve price imposed by the seller, and the right of any seller to bid either personally or through another person who may be the Auctioner.

No lots may be removed without payment of the full purchase price, and cheques cannot be accepted from purchasers unknown to the Auctioneers, without a Banker's reference.

Every lot is sold with all faults and errors, and the Auctioneers disclaim, for themselves and for the Vendor, all responsibility for authenticity, age, origin, condition or quality. All statements on such matters are statements of opinion, and not representations of fact.

Purchasers are deemed to have satisfied themselves on authenticity, condition, etc., before bidding. Each lot will become the property of the Purchaser from the fall of the hammer.

Lots uncleared by the stipulated time will be sold by Auction or Private Treaty, without notice to the former Purchaser, and the deficiency if any, by such second sale, together with all charges attending the same, shall be made good by the defaulter.

There are also conditions for clearing times which vary under differing circumstances. Some auctioneers request a deposit on first purchase although not many do these days.

Note: Conditions are usually printed in the catalogue or displayed in a prominent position in the saleroom. There is nothing in them really to deter or worry you.

There has always been talk about 'rings' and there is no doubt that such things happen. A group of people can get together and select certain articles in the catalogue, (usually in the high value range), in which they are interested. The system is that one person is selected to bid while the others refrain and therefore competition is reduced. As a result, the items can be bought at a lower price. After the sale, members of the group hold their own little auction, bidding against each other. The highest bidder claims the item. The difference between the genuine auction price and the ring price is placed in a pool. In the end, the pool is shared between all members. Therefore, some members of the ring might not actually buy anything, but will go away with money in pocket. That is the simple way it works. It cannot affect you as an ordinary buyer, for you bid your limit and buy or not, as the case may be. However, it does affect the vendor and the auctioneer. The former gets a lower price while the latter loses some of his commission as a result.

The forming of a 'ring' is illegal, forbidden by an Act of Parliament, and this Act is normally displayed in the saleroom, usually near the rostrum. Its main clause reads:

(c) If any Dealer agrees to give, or gives, or allows any gift or consideration to any other person as an inducement or reward for abstaining, or for having abstained, from bidding at a Sale by Auction generally or for any particular lot, or if any person agrees to accept, or accepts, or attempts to obtain from any Dealer any such gift or consideration as aforesaid, he shall be guilty of an offence under this Act, and shall be liable on summary conviction to a fine not exceeding one hundred pounds, or a term of prisonment for any period not exceeding six months, or to both such fine and imprisonment.'

It can be generally said that ordinary members of the public attending a sale would not be aware if a 'ring' is in operation. It would not in any case affect their purchasing a lot. In these days, with knowledge more widely spread and a greater number of dealers than there was some years ago, people forming a ring do not fare as well as they used to. So you really have nothing to worry about and can look forward to some very pleasant days attending and buying at auction.

How can the antiques and valuables in the home be best protected against loss?

The security of the premises must be considered as a first precaution. Many houses are fitted with 'Yale' type slam locks, which present little difficulty to anyone intent on making an entry. All doors should be fitted with double lever locks and special fasteners are available for windows. Locks on internal doors can slow the progress of a thief and are a deterrent, for speed is the essence — quickly in, quickly out is their rule. It is not generally known that police areas have a special officer, who will on request visit your home and advise on security. There are specialist firms who will estimate for making your home secure. No matter how many locks, the determined villain will make an entry, so do not attract him by displaying valuable silver where it can be seen by anyone passing the front window. It is impossible, (if you want to enjoy your home), to hide everything out of sight, so insurance is important.

I have frequently discovered homes to be inadequately covered. This saves premiums, which is all very well until disaster strikes and a claim is presented. In many cases, the policy does not cover the type of loss sustained. For example a workman or other person visiting your home or accidental breakage, may well not be covered by a general policy. Insurance may sound expensive, but only if you have no reason to claim. In fact, property and chattel cover is by far the cheapest form. Compare it with your car insurance, as an example. The premium paid on a car would cover your home for many thousands of pounds. It is not sufficient to think of a number and take up a general policy; discuss the matter with your broker; he will advise on the types of protection you require, such things as all risks, or even what is termed a 'duster' cover are important. Insurers often demand some security precautions to be made, so be prepared to fit additional safeguards.

Over the years receipts get lost and in any case most values rise, particularly with antiques, silver and jewellery. A ten year-old receipt would hardly support a claim with present day values. General furniture, clothing and the like, do not present much problem, but antiques and other valuables require special attention. The best safeguard is a Valuation Inventory, prepared by a specialist, who is recognised by the Insurance Companies. One copy of the Inventory should be placed with the Insurers for use in the event of claim. This ensures that they receive an adequate premium, and your claims trouble free. Such Inventories should be revised from time to time. They are also useful for family division and can be suitably adapted in the event of Probate, at a fraction of the original cost of preparation.

It is not sufficient to hold a policy; it must be the correct one for your needs. If you own a house, it must be properly insured, and subsidence, tempest and flood require to be mentioned. It is as well, when arriving at a replacement figure for the building, to bear in mind that, if the structure is destroyed the land remains, so does not have to be repurchased. Professional advice is easy to obtain, and often well worth the fees. We all have to leave our homes unoccupied at some time; better to do it with peace of mind.

Bibliography

Encyclopaedia of British Pottery and Porcelain Marks, Geoffrey Godden, Barrie and Jenkins 1970

E. Benezit, *Dictionary Peintres and Sculpteurs*, Librairie Grund 1948

English Goldsmiths and their Marks, Charles Jackson, Dover Publications 2nd Ed. 1948

Commemorative Pottery 1780/1900, John and Jennifer May, Heinemann

Tonbridge and Scottish Souvenir Woodwork, G. Bell and Sons 1970

Art and Antiques Weekly Magazine, 181 Queen Victoria Sreet, London

Victorian China Fairings, W.S. Bristowe, Adam and Charles Black

Marks and Monograms on European and Oriental Pottery and Porcelain, William Chaffers (Edited by Geoffry Godden), William Reeves 1965

Eighteenth Century English Porcelain, George Savage, Spring Books 1952

Maps and Prints, D.C. Gohm, John Gifford Ltd 1964

Dolls and Doll Makers, Mary Hillier, Weidenfield and Nicholson 1968

Doulton Pottery from the Lambeth and Burslem Studios, R. Dennis 1975

Royal Worcester Porcelain, Henry Sandon, Barrie and Jenkins 1975

The Victorian Staffordshire Figure, Anthony Oliver, Heinemann 1971

British Firemarks and Plates, Chartered Insurance Institute 1971

The Furniture Designs of Chippendale, Hepplewhite and Sheraton, Arthur Hayden, Cresset Press 1938

Paperweights, E.M. Elville, Spring Books 1967

English House Clocks, Anthony Bird, David and Charles

Investing in Georgian Glass, Ward Lloyd, Barrie and Jenkins

English Painted Enamels, Therle and Bernard Hughs, Spring Books

World Furniture, edited by Helena Hayward, Paul Hamlyn 1965

The Collectors Encyclopaedia of Antiques, edited by Phoebe Phillips, The Connoiseur 1973

Furniture Treasury, Wallace Nutting, The Macmillan Company 1969

Dictionary of Victorian Painters, Christopher Wood, Antique Collectors Club, Woodbridge, Suffolk 1971

Watch Makers and Clockmakers of the World, G.H. Baille, N.A.G. Press 1966

Index